D1502421

Vidor High School Library
Vidor, Texas 77662

WAR IN VIETNAM

BOOK IV — Fall of Vietnam
By David K. Wright

7316

Vidor High School Library
Vidor, Texas 77662

A-9875

CHILDRENS PRESS ®

CHICAGO

A Vietnamese family tries to move its ox cart out of the path of oncoming U.S. 173rd Airborne Division tanks near Trung Lap, South Vietnam.

Library of Congress Cataloging-in-Publication Data

Wright, David K.
  War in Vietnam. (The fall of Vietnam) / by David K. Wright.
    p.   cm.
  Includes index.
  Summary: Examines the conflict in Vietnam, with an emphasis on the final few years, the withdrawal of American troops, and the fall of South Vietnam.
  ISBN 0-516-02289-X
  1. Vietnamese Conflict, 1961-1975—Juvenile literature. [1. Vietnamese Conflict, 1961-1975.] I. Title. II. Title: Fall of Vietnam.
DS557.7.W73   1988   88-11104
959.704′3—dc19   CIP
                                            AC

Childrens Press®, Chicago
Copyright ©1989 by Regensteiner Publishing Enterprises, Inc.
All rights reserved. Published simultaneously in Canada.
Printed in the United States of America.
  2 3 4 5 6 7 8 9 10 R 97 96 95 94 93 92 91 90

Contents

Foreword

Vietnam. The land, the war, the experience continue to haunt the nation. It was the first war America lost, and lost causes always seem to leave more questions than answers. The four-volume series *War in Vietnam* by David K. Wright looks at why the United States became involved, why we fought the war the way we did, and why we lost. In seeking answers to these questions, Mr. Wright contributes to the healing of the nation, which remains the unfinished business of the war.

In Book I—*Eve of Battle*, Wright describes the early history of Vietnam up to the critical year 1965, when the first U. S. combat troops arrived in South Vietnam. We learn of Vietnam's long tradition of fierce independence, the period of French rule over the country, the first French-Indochina war involving the nationalist Viet Minh, and the growing American involvement following the French defeat in 1954. Wright shows us how America's entanglement deepened step by step. By 1965 the leaders in Washington, D. C., felt they had no choice but to send U. S. combat troops to save Vietnam from communism. *Eve of Battle* reveals the danger of making important national decisions without really understanding the nature and history of the people we have pledged to support.

Book II—*A Wider War* explores one of the most puzzling questions of the conflict. Why couldn't the United States—the world's greatest military power—defeat a poorly equipped peasant army? Some argue that America's politicians would not use the military force necessary to win. But *A Wider War* shows that the amount of force Americans used was much greater than in any other war. Such firepower and violence—from the smallest infantry unit to the giant B-52 bombers—turned the Vietnamese peasants against the U. S. It turned many Americans against the war as well. To these people, including some Vietnam veterans, it appeared that time was on the enemy's side. Before long, many in America lost patience with this long, costly, and savage war.

Book III—*Vietnamization* tells of the events that followed the 1968 election of Richard Nixon as President. Even though Nixon had pledged to seek "peace with honor," he pursued a complex and at times dishonest policy in running the war. In violation of the law, Nixon ordered U.S. troops to invade Cambodia and Laos. We also learn how he promised to reduce the number of U. S. troops in Vietnam yet still increase support for the South Vietnamese Army. He stepped up the bombing of North Vietnam at the same time he began secret talks with the enemy in Paris. This book also wrestles with the agonizing question of how American soldiers could have taken part in the March 1968 massacre of innocent Vietnamese civilians. The My Lai 4 incident, in which hundreds of men, women, and children were murdered, remains a black mark against America's honor. The book concludes with the heavy Christmas bombing of North Vietnam in December 1972 and with the January 1973 cease-fire agreement. The treaty ended American involvement in Vietnam but did not end the war.

The final book—*The Fall of Vietnam*—recounts the tragic consequences of America's confused policies in Vietnam. In our efforts to bring democracy and freedom to this far-away nation, we nearly lost sight of these values at home. The Watergate political scandal showed that even President Nixon and his close advisers were willing to break the law to stay in power. Richard Nixon became the only President in history forced to resign in disgrace. In one sense he can be counted as a victim of Vietnam. More tragic victims were the populations of North and South Vietnam, Cambodia, and Laos. Many U. S. Vietnam veterans also remain troubled victims of the war. No one can predict when the agony will end for the families of MIAs—those reported missing in action from 1965 to 1973. These families have waited for years to hear some word about the fate of their loved ones.

Vietnam is a sad chapter in the nation's history. The series *War in Vietnam* will help readers find answers to many of their questions about the war. The biggest question of all may be—Was Vietnam an isolated, regrettable event, or did our conduct of the war reveal the darker side of the American character? The answer to this question, perhaps more than any other, has meaning for the nation's future.

Frank A. Burdick
*Professor of History at
State University College
Cortland, New York*

A Vietnam Timeline: Major Events in the Fall of Vietnam

1973

January 27: An agreement is reached between the United States and North Vietnam to end the war in South Vietnam.

March 29: The last U.S. troops leave South Vietnam. The only Americans left behind are 8,500 civilians, plus embassy guards and a small number of soldiers in a defense office.

April 5: The U.S. Senate votes 88-3 to forbid aid to Vietnam without congressional approval.

August 15: The bombing of Cambodia by American planes ends. President Nixon criticizes Congress for ending the air war.

October 16: Henry Kissinger and Le Duc Tho are awarded the Nobel Peace Prize for ending the war in Indochina. Tho turns down the award because, as he points out, fighting continues.

1974

April 4: The U.S. House of Representatives

U.S. Marines board a troop ship in Danang Harbor, South Vietnam.

rejects a White House proposal for more aid to South Vietnam.

August 9: Richard M. Nixon resigns as President of the United States. His resignation stops impeachment proceedings. Vice President Gerald Ford is sworn in as President.

1975

January 6: The province of Phuoc Long, only 60 miles north of Saigon, is captured by the communists.

March 14: President Nguyen Van Thieu decides to pull his troops out of the central highlands and northern provinces.

April 8: A huge U.S. cargo plane, loaded with Vietnamese orphans, crashes on takeoff near Saigon. More than 100 children die.

April 17: Cambodia falls to the Khmer Rouge (Cambodian communists).

April 30: Saigon falls to the NVA and VC.

December 3: Laos falls to the Pathet Lao (Laotian communists).

John Dean III, a White House aide, prepares to testify in the U.S. Senate Watergate investigation.

1976

July 2:   The two Vietnams are officially reunified.

November 2:   James Earl (Jimmy) Carter is elected President of the United States.

1977

January 21:   President Carter pardons 10,000 draft evaders.
Throughout the year: more refugees ("boat people") leave Vietnam by any means available. Many are ethnic Chinese who fear persecution from Vietnamese victors.

1978

December: Vietnamese forces occupy a large area of Cambodia.

1979

February 17:   China invades Vietnam and is in the country for three weeks.

November 24:   The U.S. General Accounting Office indicates that thousands of Vietnam veterans were exposed to the herbicide known as

An American prisoner of war is greeted by his family after his release in 1973.

Agent Orange. The veterans claim they have suffered physical and psychological damage from the exposure.

1980

Summer: Vietnamese forces pursue Cambodians into Thailand.

November 4: Ronald Reagan is elected President of the United States.

1982

November 13: The Vietnam Veterans' Memorial is dedicated in Washington, D.C.

1984

May 7:   Seven U.S. chemical companies agree to an out-of-court settlement with Vietnam veterans over damage the veterans suffered from the herbicide Agent Orange. The settlement is for $180 million.

July 15:   Major fighting breaks out along the Vietnam-China border.

A Vietnamese soldier walks down a street in Hanoi in 1985. The war had been over for ten years.

Chapter 1

Vietnam Without Americans

The treaty signed by the United States and North Vietnam on January 27, 1973, was quite simple. It called for a cease-fire, for the withdrawal of American armed forces, and for the exchange of all U.S. and North Vietnamese prisoners of war. It did not solve the differences between the North and South Vietnamese, but it allowed the last U.S. soldier to leave Vietnam on March 29, 1973.

U.S. embassy guards stayed, along with the staff of a small defense office and an estimated 8,500 American civilians. But the fighting units were gone. America continued to supply South Vietnam with money, weapons, ammunition, and food. The contribution in U.S. lives ended in 1973. American deaths reached some 58,000, though this number has changed several times as soldiers were added to—and even a few subtracted from—the total. North Vietnam lost almost one million people. South Vietnam losses totaled 186,000 dead. Slightly over 5,000 Koreans, Australians, New Zealanders, and Thais died in the fighting.

The number of wounded always exceeds the number killed in a war, and Vietnam was no different. U.S. armed forces reported that 313,616 troops were wounded, about half of them seriously. South Vietnamese wounded totaled half a million. The number of wounded among the North Vietnamese Army (NVA) and Viet Cong guerrillas may have been about eight million. Korean, Australian, New Zealand, and Thai wounded numbered about 30,000. Total deaths and injuries among civilians are unknown. In places where the war

A Vietnamese peasant passes a rusting American tank near Cu Chi, Vietnam. The last U.S. combat soldier left South Vietnam in 1973.

was fought amid civilians, such as in Hué, casualties were very high. People were killed and wounded not only in the fighting but for political reasons as well.

Compared to the waste in human lives, the waste in dollars seems unimportant. Yet the figures are staggering by any scale. The United States alone spent $150 billion in Vietnam. Those dollars are directly connected to the war and do not include a sum almost as large for various public works and aid projects aimed at helping South Vietnamese civilians. Nor does it account for the millions spent trying to patch together the minds and bodies of the soldiers and refugees who survived the war. Added to this are the costs of benefits, such as the GI Bill, paid to soldiers or their families. The largest expense of all may be the damage that was done to the U.S. economy by the war. The conflict kept the economy artificially prosperous for so long that the country experienced both inflation and a lack of growth afterward. Veterans received no welcoming ceremonies and found few job openings. Experts in many areas still wonder whether the exact cost of the war—in lives and in dollars—will ever be known.

The presence of the United States in South Vietnam wrecked the Vietnamese economy as well. Even so, a former Saigon refugee who now lives in Westminster, California, says the mood in South Vietnam after the 1973 Paris peace accord was strangely optimistic. "We thought the agreement was better for the other side, but our army made some important gains during that time. And during the 1968 and 1972 offensives, the other side had withdrawn both times." Both sides continued to fight after they had agreed to a cease-fire. They did so because each wanted to hold as much territory as possible. The South Vietnamese controlled three fourths of their country and fought well. Yet several things happened that hurt their chances of victory.

In July 1973, the U.S. Navy obeyed the peace accord by removing mines from Haiphong and other North Vietnamese harbors. These reopened ports could now unload ships that had been unable to dock for more than a

Vietnam was still divided into two countries when American troops departed.

year. Fresh supplies were quickly taken down the Ho Chi Minh Trail through Laos and Cambodia. The trail itself had undergone recent, dramatic changes. U.S. bombing had stopped in Laos and would stop in August in Cambodia. So the trail was widened and paved in some parts, which meant it could support truck traffic. Instead of months, it now took only two weeks to move men and supplies into battle. Equally important, the North Vietnamese constructed a petroleum pipeline that ran the length of both Vietnams. This meant they had fuel for their Soviet-made battle tanks.

However, additional aid was not easy for the North to get. The Chinese and Russians were less interested in Vietnam now that the U. S. had departed. In the fall of 1973, Prime Minister Pham Van Dong and diplomat Le Duan came home from Moscow and Beijing without the extra aid they felt they needed. Meanwhile, in South Vietnam, President Nguyen Van Thieu's party had won a sweeping victory in the national elections. Thieu jailed protesting Catholics, Buddhists, and members of other faiths.

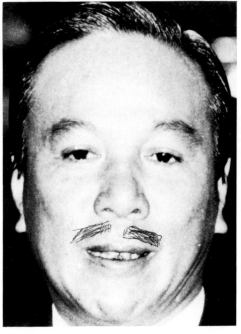

Nguyen Van Thieu.

These and other groups despised the corruption in Thieu's government. Many South Vietnamese found their hopes for a true democracy fading quickly.

Between the January cease-fire and October 1973, North Vietnam moved 70,000 troops into the South. These soldiers gathered in parts of the country controlled by the communists: the northwest and along the borders with Laos and Cambodia. In November 1973, North Vietnamese foot soldiers and Soviet-made tanks overran two Army of the Republic

Cambodians seek shelter as fighting takes place near Neak Luong on the Mekong River early in 1975.

of Vietnam camps near the Cambodian border. President Thieu pointed out that the war had begun again and sought extra aid from the United States. Congress was in no mood to provide more aid than South Vietnam had already been given. President Richard M. Nixon was about to be caught up in a political scandal that started with a break-in at the Democratic party headquarters in the Watergate apartment-hotel complex. The scandal took his attention from Vietnam and soon forced him to resign.

President Thieu had a wealth of problems as well. After the U.S. left, there were no jobs for the millions of people who were crowded into cities. Afraid to return to their villages, these refugees had survived by serving American soldiers and civilians.

There was no industry in which they could work after 1973. International aid groups took on the job of feeding these people, who lived in terrible conditions in streets and alleys. Also in great need were the many disabled Vietnamese veterans. They most often begged, showing their amputations and other scars in hope of sympathy. Soldiers knew these beggars had once been ARVN members. That, together with the fact that troops weren't always paid, contributed to Thieu's decline. So did the actions of Thieu and his friends and relatives. They made and hid fortunes by selling supplies given to them by the United States. No wonder Thieu feared being overthrown!

To make matters worse, Congress passed a law stating that no more than a billion dollars in military aid would be sent to South Vietnam for the 11 months following July 1974. Gerald Ford, who became President after Nixon resigned, assured the South Vietnamese that they would get adequate supplies. Almost immediately, the U.S. House of Representatives reduced the figure to $700 million.

Some American support troops stayed in South Vietnam after 1973.

The Vietnamese eventually saw less than $300 million in ammunition, fuel, food, and other goods. The new U.S. ambassador to South Vietnam, Graham Martin, tried to reassure President Thieu; but Congress refused Martin's pleas for more American support.

Most Americans tried to forget about South Vietnam when the final U.S. soldier departed. Newspapers and radio and television networks cooperated by closing their Saigon bureaus or by reducing their once-large staffs to one or two correspondents. The fighting went on; but because young Americans were no longer getting killed, the U.S. lost interest. In the year following the cease-fire, the South Vietnamese lost 13,788 soldiers. Communist deaths were put at 45,000. The flow of men and weapons from Hanoi never ceased as the war grew more brutal.

After the summer rainy season in 1974, the communists launched attacks on a number of South Vietnamese bases. The first areas under fire were in the Mekong Delta, where the Viet Cong had always been strong. To disable South Vietnam's huge air force,

Many Americans believed President Thieu of South Vietnam was indecisive and corrupt.

A South Vietnamese woman and several children flee communist rocket and artillery fire on the northern outskirts of Saigon.

the enemy attacked airbases regularly. The large base at Danang was illuminated almost every night by the flash and fire of rockets. Artillery began to pound South Vietnamese locations as the communists moved many large Russian guns down the Ho Chi Minh Trail. The guns were part of a new batch of weapons from the U.S.S.R. Soviet relations with America were poor, so the Soviets took pleasure in seeing a U.S. ally squirm. The Russians also wanted to be the major influence in Viet-nam and were pleased that China and the North Vietnamese were no longer good friends.

The first large enemy attack came at Phuoc Binh, a provincial capital 60 miles northwest of Saigon. The fighting began in December during the height of the dry season. On December 26, the communists seized a major road junction leading directly to Saigon. This meant that Phuoc Binh was surrounded; no ammu-nition or food could be hauled from the capital to the fighting

Henry Kissinger, left, representing the U.S., and Le Duc Tho, representing North Vietnam, held lengthy peace talks in Paris.

ARVN soldiers. Airborne rangers, some of South Vietnam's best troops, were taken by helicopter into the half-destroyed city. The defenders, though outnumbered 8,000 to 2,000, fought well. They were finally defeated in January 6 by superior numbers, dozens of tanks, and long-range artillery.

After a lull in the fighting early in 1975, the North Vietnamese turned their attention to the central highlands. The communists had massed more than 100,000 troops on the border with Laos. They attacked the city of Pleiku, then waited for the South Vietnamese to rush toward the fighting with all available troops. When the NVA was assured that South Vietnamese ARVN units had reached Pleiku and nearby Kontum, they surrounded a provincial capital to the south named Ban Me Thuot. By this time in the war, the communists were the ones with sophisticated weapons. They used flame throwers, tanks, and large artillery to take the center of Ban Me Thuot in one long day of fighting.

ARVN soldiers and local forces were pushed into a ring around the city, then attacked from behind by even more NVA units. South Vietnamese airborne troops once again were brought in and once again failed to take back Ban Me Thuot. The South could no longer call in U.S. B-52 bombers, and their own planes and helicopters were falling apart from lack of maintenance.

President Thieu took dramatic action. On March 10, 1975, he decided to pull all forces out of the central highlands and regroup them along the coast and in important areas farther south. Commanders in Pleiku were notified of the pullback. They began a withdrawal without telling anyone else. Government officials, who knew the enemy wanted them dead, were left unprotected. The U.S. embassy learned of the pullback and tried to notify American missionaries, intelligence employees, and other civilians. Most Americans were flown out of the highlands. They were among the lucky few to leave unharmed.

A military honor guard carries the casket of a U.S. airman who died in 1972 in Laos. MIAs—servicemen missing in action—continue to haunt the nation's conscience.

Chapter 2

Problems: Watergate and Selective Service

By a strange turn of events, a "second-rate burglary," committed in Washington, D.C., in 1972, played a part in the defeat three years later of the South Vietnamese. The burglars were caught in June inside Democratic Party national headquarters. The Democratic offices were in an apartment-hotel complex called Watergate. Five burglars and two men employed by President Richard M. Nixon's Committee to Re-elect the President were brought to trial.

All seven were convicted by a federal judge, John J. Sirica, who offered short sentences in exchange for more information. Judge Sirica learned that the seven had been told to keep silent and to plead guilty by White House staff members. This led to charges against more and more of Nixon's close friends and advisers. Even though the President won the 1972 election, his victory did not stop the investigation. The cover-up—the attempt to hide any connection between the burglary and the White House—stayed in the news.

In February 1973, the U.S. Senate began to investigate the Watergate matter. Senator Sam Ervin of North Carolina was picked to head a committee of Democrats and Republicans to probe the many disturbing questions that kept surfacing. Under the glare of television lights, the committee demanded answers to those questions from numerous White House staff members and Nixon friends. Presidential advisers H.R. Haldeman and John D. Ehrlichman resigned, and John Dean was fired by Nixon. In April 1973, the President told the nation on television that he was

Senator Sam Ervin of North Carolina conducted the Watergate probe.

John J. Sirica, U.S. District Court judge, handed out stiff sentences to the convicted Watergate criminals.

responsible for the entire affair, even though he had had no knowledge of it. Senators continued asking, "What did the President know, and when did he know it?"

The answers to those questions were on tape recordings of conversations made in 1972 by the White House. Richard Nixon realized the tapes could prove him guilty, and he refused to give them up. There followed a confrontation with Congress that was decided against the President. The U.S. Supreme Court ordered Nixon to give the tapes to a special prosecutor. Throughout 1973 and into 1974, as the South Vietnamese looked to the U.S. for aid, they found themselves dealing with a troubled President. Richard Nixon had made written promises to President Thieu that American support would continue. Now Nixon was more concerned with saving his presidency and less concerned with the worsening situation in Vietnam.

Tape recordings showed that the President had a secret list of his "enemies." These so-called foes were famous people who had opposed him at one time or another. Or they were "guilty" of the crime of being Democratic party members! The list even included popular actors Bill Cosby and Paul Newman. Almost as strange was the behavior of presidential adviser Henry Kissinger. He told the President that he would remain loyal, then talked about Nixon's antics behind the President's back.

Gradually, many of Nixon's congressional friends either decided he was guilty or simply quit talking about the Watergate affair. Senator Ervin's committee listened to the White House tapes and voted to impeach President

H.R. Haldeman (left) and John Ehrlichman, two aides to President Richard M. Nixon, proved to be part of a White House conspiracy.

The U.S. Senate Watergate hearings were closely followed by the nation on national television.

Nixon. He was charged with three crimes connected with obstructing justice. Nixon's illegal decision in 1969 to secretly bomb the neutral country of Cambodia was not even mentioned. Nixon admitted that he tried to sidetrack the Watergate investigation, and he resigned as President on August 9, 1974. It was the rainy season in Vietnam. The North Vietnamese and the Viet Cong were resupplying themselves, preparing to attack once the monsoon rains were over.

Nixon's problems affected the war in Vietnam in several important ways:

• He made repeated, written promises to President Thieu that American aid would be almost endless but Thieu saw little of it. Not until Gerald Ford was sworn in to succeed Nixon did Thieu finally realize no aid would come.

• His resignation led to the defeat of several South Vietnam supporters in Congress. These Republicans lost elections in the fall of 1974 because they stayed loyal to Nixon too long. Some would have worked for last-minute aid to President Thieu in 1975.

• The bombing of Cambodia

President Gerald Ford's pardon of ex-President Richard Nixon draws protests from a crowd in Pittsburgh. Historians believe the pardon may have cost Ford the 1976 presidential election.

was stopped by Congress on August 15, 1973. A stronger President, one not troubled by criminal investigations, might have challenged the congressional act.

• It's also possible that President Nixon would have ordered U.S. fighting men back to Vietnam after the so-called cease-fire in 1973 did not work. He could not even consider such a controversial action with Watergate on his mind.

After Nixon's resignation, Gerald Ford was immediately sworn in as President. He had replaced Spiro T. Agnew as Vice President in 1973. Agnew had been convicted of bribery and had resigned in disgrace. Ford quickly pardoned Nixon of any crimes he might have committed in office. The pardon came only a month after Nixon's resignation, and the action angered many people. They wondered if Richard Nixon and Ford had made some sort of secret agreement, trading Nixon's resignation for a full pardon. Whether this was true or not, pardoning Richard Nixon may have cost Ford the election in 1976.

One million young men and their families found the pardon especially unfair. These were the men who had broken federal draft laws during the war years. Many had refused to sign up with the Selective Service system (also known as the draft) at the age of 18. Some had gone to Canada when the order to report to the military arrived in the mailbox. Still others had gone into the service and then decided that the war was not for them. They deserted. By the end of the war there were 432,000 deserters, less than half the number of draft-law violators. Many of their stories were dramatic, such as the one John David Herndon could tell.

John David Herndon was a high school dropout, a wounded and decorated U.S. Army sergeant, and a paratrooper who had completed one 12-month tour of Vietnam. He was also a man who, at the age of 25, did not want to return to Vietnam. He said he believed the war was morally wrong. He deserted his post in West Germany to go to France. The West Virginian then decided to return to the United States and was helped by Safe Return, one of several groups formed to help deserters and draft dodgers. The

Gerald R. Ford

Gerald R. Ford, Jr. (born July 14, 1913), 38th U.S. President

On October 12, 1973 Gerald Ford was nominated by President Richard M. Nixon to be Nixon's Vice President. The vice presidency became vacant when Spiro Agnew was convicted of taking bribes during his term as Governor of Maryland. Ford, a long-time U.S. representative, was quickly approved by Congress.

Ford became the President automatically after Nixon resigned on August 9, 1974. A month later, he pardoned the President of all crimes and angered many Americans who felt Nixon had violated the law. They remembered this pardon in 1976 when they voted for Jimmy Carter over Ford.

The President ordered the airlift in April 1975 that brought 237,000 Vietnamese refugees to the U.S. as communists closed in on Saigon. A few weeks later, he sent the Marines to Cambodia after an American ship was seized by the Khmer Rouge. The ship and crew of 39 were retrieved, but 41 Marines died and 50 were wounded in the poorly conceived attack.

After the 1976 election, Ford retired from political office. He remains a prominent member of the Republican party.

power of the antiwar movement lined up with Herndon in part because he wasn't a wealthy college graduate but rather an everyday person.

The Army learned of Herndon's willingness to stand trial and of his combat record. The former sergeant was quietly handed a bad-conduct discharge for a minor offense the Army said he committed earlier in Germany. This was typical of the way the military reacted to desertions during the Vietnam era; in an earlier war, Herndon might have been sentenced to a prison term or executed. But in the 1960s, if a soldier said he deserted for moral or religious grounds, the government often found a way to discharge him without a trial.

Nothing occupied the minds of young people more during the Vietnam era than did the draft. If a 19-year-old was about to be drafted, he found himself unable to get a job. He could not borrow money or do many of the things adults can do. College students, high school graduates, and dropouts found ways to avoid the draft. Not everyone avoided it, however, or even tried. A small

Young Chicagoan registers for the draft in a post office in 1980. The end of the Vietnam War reduced controversy surrounding military service.

town in rural upper Michigan had 11 boys in a high school graduating class who all joined the military in the same year. Every one of these boys was killed later in Vietnam.

Draft boards, made up of local people, could determine how many local men were sent off. For example, Texas had 7 percent of the U.S. population and 4 percent of those in the military. Michigan had 4 percent of the population but 7 percent of those in the armed forces.

U.S. troop strength in Vietnam reached its peak in the spring of 1969. One year later, draft laws were changed. A national lottery system was created. The federal government said a lottery would make the draft more fair. Officials hoped it might stem the tide of young men who dodged the draft. The government also believed that making the draft less controversial would decrease opposition to the war.

Here is how the new system worked: All potential draftees were assigned a number drawn by chance. That number was based on their date of birth. For example, all 19-year-olds with a birth-

A Vietnam war deserter ponders his next move after President Jimmy Carter

day of January 4 could be in the 193rd group to be called up that year. Those men with birthdates matched to numbers 250 through 365 did not have to worry much about being called. This did not make the draft more fair; some people could still receive deferments. But it made the draft *appear* to be fair.

The new system had mixed results. During 1972, some boards in California reported that one out of every three draftees was still not showing up for induction.

Within hours of the cease-fire in 1973, the draft was stopped. There was no talk of amnesty (forgiveness) for draft dodgers. Nixon denounced amnesty, while his administration began to recruit soldiers for an all-volunteer army. In 1974, President Ford announced that draft dodgers could earn their way back into society by performing two years of work in a

pardoned Americans who had violated draft laws.

hospital or prison or other low-paying public institution. Those who had evaded the draft boycotted the plan, which eventually failed. Only 6 percent of eligible persons bothered to apply. Meanwhile, the Ford administration was having problems getting young men to register with the Selective Service. On March 29, 1975, all draft laws were temporarily suspended.

The big news for draft resisters, however, came early in 1977. Newly elected President Jimmy Carter issued a Presidential Pardon. It excused all men who had violated Selective Service laws since 1964. Military leaders followed the pardon with a program that changed the discharges of thousands of soldiers from "dishonorable" to "honorable."

The all-volunteer military was not able to meet all planned manpower needs. But it did a lot to quiet antimilitary feeling among young men and their parents. In 1979, the U.S. House of Representatives authorized the President to begin registration once again of all 18-year-old men. Ronald Reagan supported that policy.

There was a small but important group that also could have faced prosecution for antiwar activity. It was made up of nine former prisoners of war (POWs) in North Vietnam. Once these men returned home, a former prisoner, Air Force Colonel Theodore Guy, accused the others of aiding the enemy. Charges were dropped after one of the nine, a man named Abel Kavanaugh, committed suicide. One of the others, Robert Chenoweth, from Portland, Oregon, finally spoke out. He said most U.S. prisoners he knew in North Vietnam were opposed to America's war involvement. The former Army sergeant denied that he had been forced to criticize his country on North Vietnamese radio. Chenoweth was honorably discharged in July 1973. He said he gave his opinions in the broadcasts but did not encourage American soldiers to desert.

North Vietnamese guards talk to American POWs held at the Ly Nam de Prison. POWs called this prison the "Hanoi Hilton."

Chapter 3

The Fall of Saigon

Armies go into battle in an orderly manner. They usually retreat any way they can. In March 1975, South Vietnamese soldiers retreated down a little-used logging road after being told to give up the central highlands. They picked the route because they feared being ambushed by the North Vietnamese on main highways. Local militias, civilians, and families of the Army of the Republic of Vietnam troops saw them leave and followed them. The North Vietnamese Army learned of the huge retreat and gave chase. Enemy tanks and artillery fired shells at the fleeing ARVN soldiers. As often as not, the death-dealing shells landed among innocent civilians or regional soldiers armed only with rifles or handguns.

This "Convoy of Tears," as it came to be known, stretched eastward for miles toward the coast. A unit of ARVN engineers was at the front so that bridges could be hastily tied together to cross streams. Thousands of people, on foot or on bicycles, ox carts, scooters, and trucks reached crossing points before the temporary bridges were ready. These teeming swarms became easy targets for North Vietnamese artillery attacks.

People died all along the 75 miles to the coast. They were killed by the heat, lack of food or water, or by shrapnel. NVA forces caught up with the convoy at several sites and killed hundreds of soldiers and civilians. ARVN Rangers set up ambushes for NVA troops and urged many civilians to flee into the jungle to help them survive a little longer. Eventually, many died in the jungle as well.

For several more days the 250,000 people in the leaderless escape continued to stumble eastward. Senior officers had abandoned the soldiers, flying safely to

An American official punches a man to keep him from boarding an overloaded airplane fleeing Nha Trang, South Vietnam, in April 1975.

the coast in helicopters. Nearly 100,000 people lost their lives in the tragic retreat.

Meanwhile, in Saigon, evacuations were beginning. On April 8, an airplane attacked the Presidential Palace. It was just one hint of enemy strength. Other hints were the strict curfew imposed by frightened South Vietnamese and news of ARVN defeats in the central highlands. Saigon residents, especially those who worked for the U.S. or South Vietnamese governments, gathered their most valued possessions and prepared to flee the capital. Americans who had grown attached to newsstand dealers or bar girls or children who lived in the streets looked for ways to get them out of Vietnam. The quickest way was by plane, but the Americans reserved most spaces for U.S. family members and officials. Barges, ships, and boats took on added value as residents looked for ways to depart. Those without any escape plans included the numerous foreigners— Frenchmen, Koreans, Filipinos, Australians—who worked in the country. They huddled around radios and scoured newspapers for the latest reports on the war. A few foreigners who loved Saigon decided to stay and take their chances.

President Thieu believed that his mission was to keep Saigon under his control. Perhaps he thought it could become a successful, independent city-state, like Hong Kong or Singapore. To maintain control, he needed more troops and supplies. So he gave up the highlands, then decided not to defend the northern cities of Hué and Danang. ARVN and Marine commanders in those areas were told to move their men to the coast, where boats would pick them up.

The plan was to move all these troops south to defend Saigon. Hué and Danang were to be surrendered without a struggle. A few senior military men wanted to stay and fight. Thieu changed his order and told the officers to hold Hué to the last man. He then decided the ancient capital should be abandoned after all. Marines and ARVN soldiers in Hué and Danang fought as they withdrew. Numerous commanders committed suicide as their platoons, companies, and battalions fell apart.

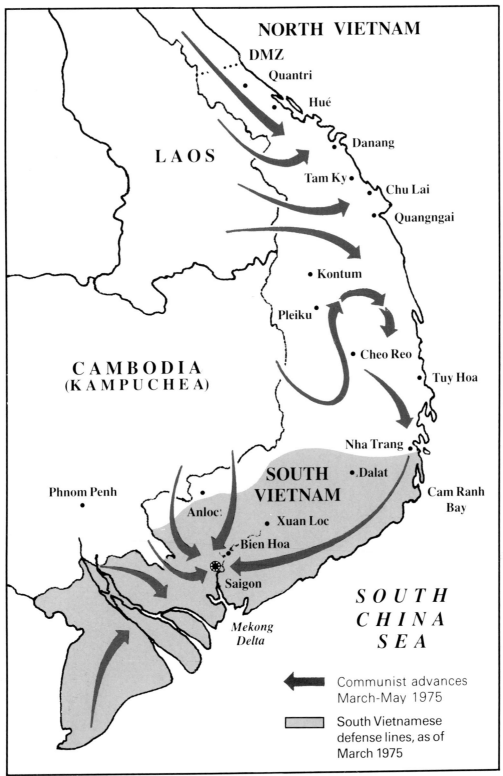

NORTH VIETNAM

DMZ

Quantri

Hué

Danang

LAOS

Tam Ky

Chu Lai

Quangngai

Kontum

Pleiku

Cheo Reo

CAMBODIA
(KAMPUCHEA)

Tuy Hoa

Nha Trang

Dalat

Phnom Penh

SOUTH
VIETNAM

Cam Ranh
Bay

Anloc

Xuan Loc

Bien Hoa

Saigon

SOUTH
CHINA
SEA

Mekong
Delta

Communist advances
March-May 1975

South Vietnamese
defense lines, as of
March 1975

Communists advanced throughout South Vietnam in the spring of 1975.

By March 31, nearly 100,000 people had fled Danang in any kind of barge or boat they could climb aboard. Word quickly reached Saigon that South Vietnam's second largest city had fallen.

Like dominoes, coastal cities to the south of Danang also fell into NVA hands. Many were given up without a shot being fired. Cam Ranh Bay, a deep-water port built by American forces, was quickly abandoned. Most people died while trying to flee. In Nha Trang, for example, refugees were crushed in the mass trying to board boats or were accidentally pushed into the sea as overloaded barges rocked in the waves. ARVN soldiers kept moving their line of defense farther south. They finally stopped at Xuan Loc, a town only 60 miles northeast of Saigon. The soldiers who remained were determined to make a stand against the North Vietnamese.

These ARVN and Airborne troops were still patriotic, despite their dislike of President Thieu. They could not understand how the South Vietnamese government could have given up the highlands, since the ARVN out-

Refugees crowd barges and sampans as Danang falls to the communists.

numbered the NVA. The North Vietnamese correctly believed that Xuan Loc was the last big obstacle before reaching Saigon. ARVN forces desperately tried to defend the town. The South flew most of their fighter and transport planes against the three NVA divisions there. Even cargo planes were used to drop bombs on the enemy. Nothing stopped the North Vietnamese for long, because they could see that the end was near. They outflanked the courageous South Vietnamese, who gave way on April 16. Survivors struggled westward into Bien Hoa, a town just 15 miles north of the capital.

U.S. Ambassador Graham Martin was the top-ranking American left in Saigon. He was to direct the evacuation of all American and key Vietnamese personnel as the enemy closed in. Martin has been criticized for not beginning evacuation earlier, perhaps as early as the end of March. He later told Congress that dramatic action by the U.S. embassy would have caused panic among the residents of Saigon. Nevertheless, the prolonged, almost leisurely evacuation meant some people

Graham Martin

Graham Martin (born September 22, 1912) U.S. ambassador to South Vietnam

Graham Martin was the U.S. ambassador to South Vietnam during that troubled country's final days. A native of North Carolina, he was known throughout his career as a hard-working, honest, and intelligent man. In Saigon in 1975, however, those qualities weren't enough.

Martin had lost a son in Vietnam. He also truly believed that America should stop communism wherever it took root. Don Luce, who wrote a book very critical of the U.S. presence in Vietnam after serving as a volunteer, recalls that Martin had a blind spot where Vietnam was concerned. "I wonder if he should have been assigned there," says Luce. "He couldn't talk to me without losing his temper and shouting."

would be left behind. Despite Martin's pleas throughout the spring of 1975, Congress did not seriously consider sending the Vietnamese more aid.

President Thieu resigned on April 20 and left the country the following day. The government was now in the hands of elderly General Duong Van Minh. The General was unusually tall for a Vietnamese (six feet, whereas most Vietnamese are around five feet or a bit more). He told anyone who would listen that he liked playing tennis and raising flowers more than running his country. Minh was simply a caretaker and not a real leader. He sat in the heavily barricaded Presidential Palace and waited for the North Vietnamese to enter the city. He did not have long to wait.

In the meantime Washington tried to buy time for the Americans and Vietnamese officials still in Saigon. They did this by asking the Soviet Union and others to remind the NVA that the remaining Americans were not soldiers. Many who wanted to leave Saigon were already at Tan Son Nhut Airbase, on the outskirts of the capital, waiting for a seat on a transport plane. Planning was so poor that some of the people waiting to leave had to break into an old military mess hall to cook what food they could find. They were still better off than the passengers on an earlier flight.

On April 8 a huge government airplane had been loaded with Vietnamese orphans and the children of Vietnamese who planned to leave the country later. The children were strapped in two to a seat and supervised by 62 adults from U.S. government and other offices. The tiny passengers were headed for the United States. Some had been assigned to Americans who waited to adopt them. Shortly after takeoff from Tan Son Nhut, the big plane lost cabin pressure. A door blew out, jamming some controls. The plane crashed into a rice paddy, killing many of the adults and 200 of the 240 children. Fortunately, this "babylift" was the only passenger aircraft to crash during the entire evacuation.

Soviet rockets crashed into Saigon on April 27, which told residents the communists were just a few miles away. People with real or imaginary ties to Ameri-

Two of 55 Vietnamese orphans arrive in Oakland, California, on one of the last commercial flights to leave Saigon.

cans began to wait across the street from the U.S. embassy. Others went to Tan Son Nhut Airbase. There they were stopped at the gate if they did not have the right papers. So they camped at the gate, watching for people they recognized who could get them on the base and out of the country. Huge C-130 transport planes were flying in and out of Tan Son Nhut with regularity. Their destination was an American base in the Philippines, where they turned around for Saigon as soon as their passengers were on the runway. Saigon residents who had found a way out on a boat were delayed briefly. A squad of enemy soldiers was firing on any boat that went

Catholic students continued to protest government corruption in South Vietnam until the country fell.

Communist rockets hit the U.S. Agency for International Development (USAID) compound in a Saigon suburb. Enemy rockets and artillery rounds slammed into the city throughout late April 1975.

down the short river toward the sea. Other residents headed for boats hidden in various inlets.

Mortars rained on the airbase on April 29. Fighting broke out among Vietnamese soldiers. They all wanted to be on a plane or helicopter out of the country. Several civilians were injured when a mortar hit the roof of the gymnasium where they were hiding. A C-130 was hit by a rocket or mortar and exploded on a taxiway. Another was hit and disabled. Outside, ARVN and Marine members tore off their clothes, afraid that they would be killed by the advancing communists.

At the U.S. embassy, a huge crowd waited for evacuation. A tree inside the grounds was cut down so helicopters could land and pick up people inside. If there were hundreds waiting inside the embassy walls, there were thousands outside trying to climb into the compound. Barefoot Vietnamese jumped from trees and light poles outside the embassy onto rolls of barbed wire atop the embassy fence. Helicopters furnished by the U.S. Central Intelligence Agency made trips back and forth from the embassy roof to American ships anchored in the South China Sea.

The last U.S. helicopter left the embassy on the morning of April 30. More than 400 Vietnamese who had been promised that they would be taken were abandoned in the embassy yard. The last Americans to leave were 11 Marines. They tossed tear gas over the sides of the embassy roof as they climbed into a helicopter. The gas prevented the angry crowd below from taking more than a few stray shots at them. That same afternoon, the first units of the North Vietnamese Army entered Saigon.

Vietnamese Marines abandon Danang. The ships headed south for the former U.S. port at Cam Ranh Bay.

Chapter 4

Horror in Cambodia, Hardship in Laos

Khmer Rouge troops walked slowly into the Cambodian capital of Phnom Penh on April 17, 1975. They carried automatic weapons and wore the checkered scarves seen all over Cambodia. The men did not return bystanders' smiles and waves. Their arrival marked the end of the final round of fighting in Cambodia.

That round began on January 1, 1975. The Khmer Rouge (Cambodian communists) steadily surrounded, rocketed, overran, and chased the troops of Premier Lon Nol. The fighting was vicious. Government forces fell back to cities and main roads, then retreated toward the capital city. Phnom Penh was without food, fuel, or ammunition from February until April. Lon Nol, disabled due to a stroke, fled to Hawaii on April 1, and U.S. Ambassador John G. Dean departed on April

12. Lon Nol's cabinet ministers decided to stay to meet the conquering Khmers. That was a decision the ministers would pay for with their lives.

President Ford and Secretary of State Kissinger had tried in vain to rally support for the Lon Nol government. Despite rumors of Khmer Rouge brutality, neither Congress nor the country wanted to assist Cambodia further. Idealistic urges to contain communism, aid the oppressed, and right all wrongs sounded stale to congressional leaders. They were more interested in helping the American economy, which was limping badly at the time. Ambassador Dean had warned of a bloodbath if the communists took over. Few paid attention since that kind of warning is made whenever a revolution takes place.

This time, the fears proved cor-

Vietnamese wait for food in "Little Saigon," part of the U.S. marine base at Camp Pendelton, California.

Vidor High School Library.
Vidor, Texas 77662

A-9875

rect. The Khmer Rouge immediately ordered everyone to leave major cities, even persons in hospital beds. They killed anyone who hesitated. About 2.5 million men, women, and children were marched into the countryside to create an entirely new society. One million died of starvation, beatings, overwork, or from being buried alive. The Khmer Rouge did not shoot many people because they wanted to save ammunition.

The new Cambodian government did other things that made little sense. They had been given arms by the North Vietnamese, yet they attacked Vietnamese soldiers and civilians along the border in May. At the same time, Khmer Rouge soldiers grabbed an American cargo ship and held its crew. U.S. Marines reclaimed the ship in heavy fighting after the crew talked their captors into letting them go free.

It appears today that the Khmer Rouge leader, Pol Pot, believed his country would not work properly until he stamped out all foreign influence. That meant killing Cambodians who spoke French or wore western clothes and wiping out villagers whose ancestors were Vietnamese. Refugees began to arrive in Thailand during the summer of 1975. Their stories were so terrible that at first no one believed them.

The horrible situation in Cambodia grew even worse. The government of what came to be called Democratic Kampuchea even turned on itself. Pol Pot tortured and killed many of his own supporters. Hundreds of Khmer Rouge members fled the country. By the end of 1977, Kampuchea and Vietnam were at war. The Khmer Rouge found itself fighting a huge army while it continued to bully, enslave, starve, and kill its own people. Vietnamese soldiers came back from fighting in Kampuchea to describe the country as "a land of blood and tears, hell on earth." The Vietnamese launched a huge attack on the country at the end of 1978. Pol Pot and his army were pushed into the hilly, rural area near the border with Thailand. A government closely allied to the Vietnamese was created and thousands of Vietnamese soldiers stayed in Kampuchea.

Today, Cambodia is little better

Cambodian President Lon Nol walks with family and officials in 1975. Cambodia and South Vietnam fell within a few days of each other.

off than before. The cities have been opened and some farmers are bringing in rice, vegetable, and fruit harvests. But there is little work in any of the towns or cities. Services such as safe drinking water or electricity hardly exist. Most Cambodians who had any kind of mechanical or professional skills are dead. Diseases such as tuberculosis, malaria, and parastic infections are as common as colds. The United Nations and other organizations continue to supply food to what has been called the poorest nation on earth. The country's most famous tourist attraction, the ancient temples of Angkor Wat, is falling apart from lack of care. Once a pretty, relaxed little country, Cambodia will take a long time to recover from the Khmer Rouge.

There were still about 150,000 Vietnamese soldiers in Cambodia in 1988. Many patrol the border with Thailand, looking for Pol Pot and his followers. The Vietnamese are also on the lookout for a small band of Cambodians who want a government that is pro-Western. Vietnam may want to keep Cambodia just as it is— without good leadership or hope.

That way, the Vietnamese won't have to worry about hostile forces on their southwestern border.

By comparison, the communist takeover in neighboring Laos was tame. Laos was a very underdeveloped country that had been ruled by a royal family for 650 years. In recent times, a three-man government made up of a communist, a rightist, and a neutralist had tried to run this country of about 3.6 million persons. But outsiders, including the U.S. and North Vietnam, supported fighting among the three leaders and their armies.

The fighting at first was subdued. Each year the communists advanced during the dry season, then retreated as the rains came. America's Central Intelligence Agency (CIA) recruited and trained many of the hill tribes. North Vietnam aided the Laotian communists, known as the Pathet Lao. Neutral forces tried to stay out of the way. This was a strange civil war. Officers on both sides fought barefoot and half dressed for a few hours each day, then met later in a marketplace to shop or drink tea!

The balance among the three

Pol Pot

Pol Pot (formerly Saloth Sar), date of birth not known, leader of Cambodian communists, 1973-1978

Pol Pot, although a communist, is distantly related to Cambodia's original royal family. He grew up in Phnom Penh, received an education in France, then went into the Cambodian countryside in 1963 as a guerrilla fighter. From 1963 on, the Khmer Rouge or Cambodian communists rallied around him.

It appears that he is most responsible for the estimated one million Cambodian deaths that took place beginning in 1975. Only a madman would kill people for living in cities or for wearing glasses or for handing out enough food for other Cambodians to survive. Pot ordered the torture and execution of many of his own countrymen.

In 1976 Pol Pot named himself prime minister of Cambodia. When Vietnam invaded Cambodia in 1978, it appeared that Vietnam would end the killing of civilians. Pol Pot fled the capital city of Phnom Penh early in 1979. He and a few thousand Khmer Rouge guerrillas are still in western Cambodia, near the Thailand border.

forces ended in 1975 when Pathet Lao troops seized the important central Plain of Jars. The opposition fled and the Vietnamese-backed Laotian communists took over. This frightened the shopkeepers, students, military officers, and foreign residents. Many left the country with their families, crossing the Mekong River into Thailand. Stores in the capital of Ventiane were shut for lack of business or goods. At the same time, a poor harvest meant that there was not enough rice to eat. Farmers became even more desperate in 1977, when a drought hit. Rice paddies that had overflowed the year before now lay cracked and barren from lack of rain. Hungry Laotians formed resistance movements or continued to leave the country. Some farmers, who at first wanted to fight the government, decided to go to Thailand. The exodus was not easy — government troops tried to kill families who wanted to cross the wide Mekong River.

While people attempted to reach Thailand, the Thais cut off the movement of all goods into Laos. This was done because Laotian soldiers had killed a Thai

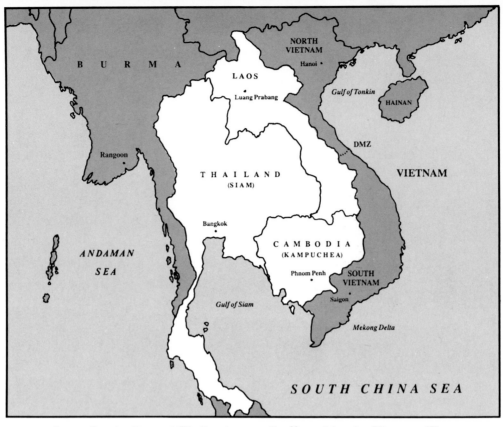

Laos, Cambodia, and Thailand were all affected by the Vietnam War.

soldier who was patroling the busy border. The value of Laotian currency fell and hunger was widespread. Since Thais living near the border share the same ancestors as the Laotians, trade was soon restored. But the situation forced the Laotian government to turn for aid to the Vietnamese and the Soviet Union. Today, Russian and Vietnamese advisers outnumber all others in Laos.

Most Laotians fleeing the country were tribespeople. Many had waged guerrilla war against the communists in Laos and in Vietnam. So the pro-communist, low-land Laotians cooperated with the North Vietnamese in ruling the Hmong and other tribes. The Hmong had their own methods of living cooperatively and did not want to be told how to share their crops of hill rice, vegetables, tobacco, and opium. They had real concerns that the new communist government would attempt to wipe them out. Fortunately, the government modified its treatment of Hmong and other minorities. However, Hmong refugees now in the U.S. indicated they felt conditions in Laos to be too dangerous for them

Montagnard tribespeople, fierce fighters who helped U.S. forces in Southeast Asia, head for resettlement after landing in Los Angeles.

to stay. Still, they miss their country. Many believe they may one day go back to Laos and liberate it from the Pathet Lao government. A few guerrillas, who hide in Thailand, still attack isolated communist soldiers.

Two Hmong now living in the U.S. confirm the strange nature of the Laotian conflict. One, a teenaged student in 1975, said the communists were especially hateful toward anyone who was in school. The Vietnamese knew that schools such as the French institution, which the young man had attended, were financed by the U.S. Central Intelligence Agency. The CIA provided schooling for children of officers in the pro-Western army. The other Hmong, at age 12, began daring rescues of downed American pilots and was wounded several times. "We could have pushed them (the communists) out of Laos many times, but we were told to stop," he says. Strange attitudes, combined with two million tons of bombs dropped on a tiny undeveloped country—will anyone ever make sense of the war that took place in Laos?

The horrors of war are bad

Cambodian refugees return from a food line with rice and water in a camp in Thailand. Millions of Cambodians of all ages were killed during Pol Pot's reign of terror.

enough, but what about the possibility of revenge after the conflict is over? What happens when the victors turn on those they've overrun? In Cambodia, events there can only be called a bloodbath. In Laos, hill people suffered while trying to escape the country. They also were sometimes attacked by North Vietnamese who were angry that the tribes had worked for the U.S. There is some evidence that the communists sprayed gas on tribespeople. The small Laotian middle class fled before the new government could kill them.

Some believe the Vietnamese want to keep Cambodia and Laos weak and dependent. Vietnam shares its northern border with a historic enemy, China. The Vietnamese may feel that weak neighbors are less worrisome than strong ones. There is no indication today that Vietnam wants to invade Thailand or Malaysia or any other Southeast Asian nation. The Chinese have become friendly with Thailand, in part because the Chinese dislike the Vietnamese. For the moment, there is a balance of power in the region.

Chapter 5

Veterans

The people of Southeast Asia were not the only ones who continued to suffer after the war was over. Many U.S. Vietnam veterans continued to carry the war within themselves even after leaving the army. One such veteran was James Bledsoe.

James was a quiet boy who grew up in Richmond, Indiana. He liked sports and became a star baseball player in a teen-age league that won a Richmond city championship in 1960. He ran on the high school track team as well. But James was not a good student. He dropped out of school in the 11th grade. When he turned 18 on August 5, 1966, and registered for the draft, the conflict in Vietnam had been going on for about two years. James moved to New York City, where he lived with his older brother, a policeman. When his draft notice came, James was 19. He was working in a laboratory and learning mechanical drafting at night.

Thousands of young men from all over the country were being trained for Vietnam. They were taken by ship or air from the West Coast to the war. James told his brothers and his parents that he did not want to go. Eventually, the military police marched him to a troop ship and he was on his way to Vietnam.

Several things happened to James in Vietnam that left a permanent mark on him. His father recalls that the Viet Cong killed a soldier as James lay asleep on the cot next to him. He saw other friends die in agony and won two Bronze Stars in heavy fighting in the central highlands. After the death of his sleeping friend, James moved into a large sewer pipe and surrounded it with sandbags. There was only one way in, and anyone who entered could be seen.

James did not write home often, which made his family suspect that there were other

Paul Oliveto, a Vietnam veteran, sits in an outpatient clinic in Hicksville, N.Y.

frightening events during his tour of duty. Fear even followed him home—on his flight from Vietnam, one of the plane's engines caught fire in the middle of the Pacific Ocean. After his discharge from the service, he couldn't seem to get his life going again. The Bledsoe family sensed his pain and said little to him when he began to drink heavily soon after he returned home. He even used drugs briefly.

Unemployed and with a bushy, reddish beard, James was nicknamed "Foxx" by his friends. He spent time in bars, babysat children, attended high school basketball games, and kept drinking excessively. Over the years the sweet wine he liked ruined his teeth. He could only drink it warm; chilled wine caused him pain. Foxx continued to refuse to sleep in a bed. Often, he slept in a friend's yard or on his father's couch. He talked about Vietnam when he was sober but was able to forget about it when he drank.

Foxx's shaky existence neared its end on March 20, 1987. He was arrested for public intoxication and taken to the Wayne County jail. His father saw him Saturday,

as he suffered from alcohol withdrawal. On Sunday morning, "he was fine." Sunday evening, he was beaten in the jail and taken to the local hospital. "His brain died in jail," said Harold Bledsoe. "His body lived until it was taken off the life-support machine." Investigations into his death by the FBI and Indiana State Police continue. James "Foxx" Bledsoe—athlete, war hero, alcoholic, friend, son and brother—was 39 years old.

Happily, James Bledsoe's story is not typical of most Vietnam veterans. "Ninety percent or more of the men who served in Vietnam have gotten on with their lives," says a spokesperson for the Veterans Administration. "But a small percentage felt that, when they were in Vietnam, they were important. They carried a gun and got attention. When they came home, life was dull once again. So they wear fatigues, talk the language, et cetera.

"There are also veterans who saw or were a part of terrible things—they suffer from post-traumatic stress. That used to be known as combat fatigue or shell shock. It is a neurosis [a mental disorder] that can occur long after

Vietnam veteran James Burdge shows a rash he claims was caused by exposure to Agent Orange. Chemical companies that produced the herbicide agreed to a $180 million settlement with the veterans.

an event. We are very good at understanding it and treating it. The Veterans Administration has placed no time limit on treating

American prisoners of war (POWs) in Hanoi.

vets with it. If a veteran says he has post-traumatic stress and we can confirm what caused it, he will be cared for.'' The VA, as it is called, would have treated James Bledsoe for his condition. But no one succeeded in getting him to go to a Veterans Administration facility.

The public often has a better opinion of Vietnam veterans than do veterans themselves. In a study paid for by the VA, Americans said the war in Vietnam was a mistake. But they blamed political leaders, not soldiers, for what happened. The public also felt that Vietnam veterans have special problems. Believe it or not, U.S. citizens who were most opposed to the war also feel the most sympathy for veterans. The vets themselves pointed out that after they returned home from the war they had problems finding a job, finding a direction in life, and finishing their education. Fewer than half of the Vietnam veterans said they were given a friendly reception when they returned.

Who are these people? Why did they serve? The study shows that most were young and poor. More than half enlisted, rather than entering through the draft. About 70 percent of the men who saw the worst combat were draftees. Most soldiers who served in Southeast Asia saw some moderate or heavy combat. Soldiers who had not completed high school were more likely to be in combat. Soldiers less than 20 years old were much more likely to be in combat than those over the age of 35. Minorities—Blacks and Latinos—were only slightly more likely to be in combat. Most veterans told the people who conducted the survey that they were proud to be vets. They said they enjoyed serving the country and would do it again if called. A significant minority, however, especially younger vets and those who saw heavy combat, disliked the military and said they would not serve again.

The attitudes expressed by Vietnam veterans reflect the unusual nature of the war. Many still feel alienated. That means they do not feel they are a part of American society. They may suffer from flashbacks; this is the sudden, vivid recall of a moment in combat or other unpleasant

POWs often were wounded before they were captured. These injuries were seldom treated while they were in prison.

Many veterans still recall the thunderous roar of tanks, artillery fire, and carpet bombings as they attempt a return to civilian life.

Worldwide unpopularity of the war affected many Vietnam vets. They often felt alienated from the civilian population.

experience that makes a person feel the event is happening all over again. Veterans believe television news stories shown during their service years portrayed them in an unfavorable way. In contrast, the majority of Americans said in the study that the newsfilms gave them a favorable impression of U.S. troops. The public, in fact, said it was more willing to support programs for veterans because of what was shown on television during the war. Employers and educators back up this favorable opinion of vets. So it appears that others do have a higher opinion of the Vietnam veteran than the vet has of himself.

Because it was a different war, it produced different veterans. These people had new kinds of problems such as drug addiction, unusual illnesses or wounds, and psychological disorders that the Veterans Administration never before had to treat. The only World War II veterans who had drug problems were those who were accidentally addicted to pain killers. Drug-dependent Vietnam vets came home by the hundreds. This, plus the fact that some vets

James Earl Carter

James Earl (Jimmy) Carter (born October 1, 1924), 39th U.S. President

Jimmy Carter fulfilled a campaign promise on January 21, 1977, his first full day as President. He pardoned young men who had evaded the draft during the Vietnam conflict. This action, together with the promised return of the Panama Canal to Panama and the U.S. hostage crisis in Iran, angered conservatives and some veterans. They and others abandoned him during the 1980 election, won by Ronald Reagan.

Carter was a U.S. Naval Academy graduate and served seven years as a naval officer. As President, however, he was neither strongly for nor against the military. Some historians believe Iran would not have taken U.S. embassy personnel hostage in 1979 if America had convincingly won the war in Vietnam. They feel that Iranian extremists stormed the embassy in Teheran because they no longer respected America's ability to strike back.

Relations with the Vietnamese improved during Carter's term. He also supported giving federal money and U.S. citizenship quickly to the Southeast Asian refugees.

regarded the VA as part of the military, made for poor communications.

It took time for the VA to meet these new problems, and some Vietnam veterans formed their own self-help groups. Working with the Carter administration, a group called Vietnam Veterans of America lobbied Congress for funds to set up better services for vets. This lobbying resulted in the creation of 189 Vet Centers across the country. These non-VA counseling sites helped the veteran deal with himself, his family, his employer, and the community. By 1988, most vets with problems had been seen by either the VA or by Vet Center personnel.

The Veterans Administration also cares for the many men who suffered severe injuries in the war. The VA sponsors research that has created the best artificial limbs known. They pay disabled veterans monthly. The amount depends on the severity of the veteran's problem. They also provide routine educational assistance, job training, loan guarantees, and burial benefits. Besides improving U.S. society through helping veterans, these VA benefits add about $500 million each year to the economy of the average state.

The most significant worry for some Vietnam veterans continues to be Agent Orange. This was an herbicide (a plant killer) used by the military in Vietnam. The name comes from the barrels in which it was stored: each one had a large orange stripe. The purpose of Agent Orange was to deny the enemy a place to hide. It was also used so that bombs and artillery could hit the ground instead of bursting harmlessly in thick treetops. The material was made in the U.S., then shipped in two parts to Southeast Asia, where it was mixed. A byproduct of this mixture was dioxin, one of the most toxic substances known.

After the war, many veterans who had handled the chemical or been accidentally sprayed became ill. Some of their children were born with severe birth defects. In 1984, a lawsuit was filed on behalf of thousands of veterans against the companies that made Agent Orange. The suit was settled out of court for $180 million by the chemical companies. They admitted no guilt and said at the time

American planes spray defoliants above a Vietnamese jungle. Agent Orange contained dioxin, which has been shown to harm humans and animals.

that there was no proof Agent Orange caused illness or death. Many veterans with cancer and other life-threatening diseases wonder if that can be true. Those with ill or deformed children usually believe Agent Orange is to blame. A spokesman for the Veterans Administration thinks any connection between Agent Orange and veterans' ailments may be impossible to prove or disprove to everyone's satisfaction.

It took years for Agent Orange to be questioned. It also took years for proper recognition of Vietnam veterans, who total about 2.8 million Americans. They returned one by one from Vietnam, leaving their units whenever their 12-month duty ended. There were no big-city parades or other salutes for them. The lack of thanks from the nation bothered many veterans. It showed dramatically in 1981, when America's hostages in Iran were given a huge parade in New York City.

Finally, on Veterans Day weekend November 13-17, 1982, a massive parade was staged in Washington, D.C. Veterans from all across America came to the capital to watch the dedication of the Vietnam Veterans Memorial. The black granite wall listed the names of 58,000 men and 8 women who died while serving in the military in Southeast Asia. Not even this 496-foot wall was without controversy. Some disliked it so much they insisted that a sculpture of combat soldiers be placed nearby. There also is a project under way to create a memorial for women who served in Vietnam. In New York City, a special part of the Intrepid Air-Sea-Space Museum notes the 238 Congressional Medals of Honor won by soldiers in Vietnam.

The story of the nation's thousands of Vietnam veterans is one of courage, frustration, troubled times, and hope. The majority of vets have been able to build satisfying lives, while a few continue their struggle to put the war behind them. A Marine veteran who lives in East Chicago, Indiana, may have said it best about his fellow vets. "A few of the guys who came back from Vietnam weren't worth much. But they were the ones who weren't worth much even before they were drafted."

A disabled Vietnam veteran searches for the name of a dead comrade on the
Vietnam War Memorial in Washington, D.C. The memorial was dedicated in 1984.

Chapter 6

The MIAs

American prisoners of war (POWs) were returned after the cease-fire in March 1973. They were thin, diseased, and dazed either by torture or by neglect. Frequently, they showed old wounds, suffered when they injured themselves bailing out of their damaged aircraft. Some of the prisoners had been in captivity more than seven years. Others were marched through hot, wet jungles and suffered from tropical illnesses. Yet they greeted their families, collected back pay, accepted promotions or a discharge, and got on with their lives.

The only sad side of the prisoner return was that many families with sons or brothers or fathers missing in action (MIAs) had no one to welcome. MIAs from the war in Vietnam were treated differently by the U.S. government. Many families—up to 2,477 at one time—have had to wonder for years if their soldier is

still alive somewhere in Indochina.

Some 1,113, or nearly half, of the MIAs are known to have been killed in action, but their bodies were not recovered. In the cases of 647 others, they were presumed dead at the time they were lost. As a result, when the war ended, fewer than 800 were regarded by the military as genuine MIAs. Many of these men were pilots whose planes were shot down. Since no parachute was sighted, it is assumed that each died in his plane. The Air Force, Navy, and Marine units have listed such pilots as missing so their families can continue to receive financial support. In 1974, after President Richard M. Nixon claimed that all prisoners had been returned, wives of MIAs picketed the White House. Many relatives, before and after the war ended, were either told nothing or told to keep quiet. This was particularly true of

U.S. Marines rescue a wounded buddy under fire. Most wounded Americans were rescued, but hundreds became MIAs—missing in action.

the men who were reported missing in Cambodia or Laos during the illegal bombing raids.

David Elder is a member of the American Friends Service Committee, an organization run by the Quakers. His group has provided everything from artificial limbs to fish hooks for Vietnamese civilians. He points out that only 4 percent of U.S. military deaths in Southeast Asia were not confirmed, compared to about 20 percent in World War II and Korea. "But the State Department would not let military leaders close the books on the MIAs, even though no one presumed dead has yet showed up alive. In World War II and Korea, MIAs were declared dead a year after the war ended. In Vietnam, that would have been January 1974. But the State Department had seen that the MIAs were a good tool for rallying public opinion."

Many relatives of the MIAs joined the National League of Families of American Prisoners and Missing in Southeast Asia. Begun in the late 1960s, the league today is concerned with the recovery of MIAs' physical remains and the possibility that there may still be live prisoners in Southeast Asia. The organization is run by Ann Mills Griffiths, whose brother is a MIA. It has been skilled at keeping the MIA issue on the minds of Americans. In fact, false hopes may have arisen from the league's efforts. The public has been encouraged to think that there are live MIAs in Southeast Asia prisons.

Facts seem to indicate otherwise. Vietnam's general secretary, Nguyen Van Linh, told *Time* magazine in September 1987, "I guarantee that there is not one single American held prisoner in our country." Earlier, Prime Minister Pham Van Dong and others said the same thing. Since 1975 there have been 2,600 reported sightings of Americans being held against their will. Yet when examined closely, only five of these reports seemed to be reliable. With such little evidence, chances are slim that a Vietnamese prison with POWs exists. Authorized and unauthorized scouting trips by Americans into Laos have produced no proof of MIAs in captivity. Many of the refugees who reported seeing Americans may actually have seen

The unpopularity of the war, as demonstrated by the peace tattoo on Sgt. John Autenrieth, complicated the issue of locating and recovering missing men.

Frenchmen. About 15,000 French citizens were in South Vietnam as late as April 1975.

Finally, the Vietnamese have no reason to hold American prisoners. They claim they did not keep any Frenchmen in prison after the French defeat in 1954. If the Vietnamese did keep prisoners, many countries that trade with Vietnam might cut off their badly needed supplies.

However, we shouldn't dismiss the hopes of the families who wait. Some information cries out for investigation. France, in fact, did pay Vietnam to get some of its prisoners back after 1954. President Nixon promised the North Vietnamese $3.5 billion for any MIAs but never followed through on his promise. A former communist named Han Vi claims there were 30 to 40 POWs in a prison in rural North Vietnam after the 1973 cease-fire. The prisoners of war who returned were told during their captivity that not all of them would be going home. A former employee of America's secretive National Security Agency has said that 302 to 304 MIAs were not returned. He said his figures are based on North Vietnamese radio traffic. It was his job to monitor these radio messages, he added. Retired General Eugene Tighe, who headed the Defense Intelligence Agency, puts the figure at between 400 and 500 missing men. Both of these men are reliable, but neither one has actually seen captive MIAs.

Some of the information that sounded best in the beginning, however, has not held up over time. Many Southeast Asian refugees claimed to have seen POWs, but those people were so eager to get out of refugee camps that they might have been willing to say anything. A Swedish engineer claimed that he saw imprisoned white men near a dam project in North Vietnam. However, he's been called a liar and a hard drinker by his friends. No one today is sure what to make of the words of former prisoner of war Robert Garwood.

Garwood was captured in 1965 and chose to stay in North Vietnam after the other POWs came home in 1973. A few years later, in 1979, he returned to the U.S. and reported rumors he had heard that he was not the last American in Vietnam. However, all prison-

Robert Garwood, captured in 1965, left the North of his own free will in 1979. Was he the last living American to depart?

ers who were known by other POWs have been accounted for. Garwood's rumors would have to be about someone held apart from all the other prisoners. Garwood was cleared by the military of charges of desertion but was convicted of collaboration, which is cooperating with the enemy. Once again, those who were hurt most by the POWs' stories were the family members who wait.

Stories from other sources also help keep the MIA issue alive. A Californian named Scott Barnes states in a book that he saw two American POWs held captive in Laos in 1981. Barnes reported that he was part of an expedition to locate MIAs and that he saw two white men, who seemed to be in their 40s, in a small prison in Laos. He said that listening devices showed the two men to be speaking English. He further wrote that, after he reported the two prisoners, he was sent back to Bangkok. The man Barnes was with, James Gritz, was a former Green Beret colonel. The Thais made him leave their country. Barnes says American intelligence officials were then sent into Laos to kill the two prisoners! This sounds terribly far fetched, but Barnes believes these MIAs were pilots who flew a supersecret mission over Laos that the U.S. never wants known. Families of MIAs and the public alike are willing to believe all kinds of reports. One critic, however, has called Barnes' book a scrapbook of other people's stories.

The League of Families has split over these and other reports. Some members, labeled the "Rambo faction," are telling the League that they should not believe too much of what the U.S. government has been telling them. These people want final proof that the MIAs are alive or dead. Others believe that the Reagan administration in particular used them to keep the country afraid of the threat of communism. Ronald Reagan had in fact said the MIAs were a high priority; but except for MIA remains, no live prisoners have turned up. Bill Paul, a *Wall Street Journal* writer, has repeatedly asked that the government offer to pay a ransom, if necessary, for any living MIAs. Vietnam leader Nguyen Van Linh has called the idea of a reward "absurd."

An increasing number of Americans believe the best way to make certain that there are no MIAs in Vietnam is for the U.S. to normalize relations with the Vietnamese. That way, U.S. citizens could obtain travel visas and visit the country in large numbers. At present, Vietnam is allowing more and more American tourists into the country, but they follow carefully guided tours. The State Department recommends against normal relations with Vietnam until Vietnamese soldiers leave Cambodia. Some troops have been pulled out, but it will be years before Cambodia is run only by Cambodians. Meanwhile, Vietnamese citizens who could benefit from American aid are deprived of it, and Americans are deprived of the certainty that all prisoners are either dead or safely home.

Two lines of U.S. prisoners await release in Hanoi in 1973. Some prisoners accused others of cooperating with the enemy.

Lt. Col. Robert L. Strim's family rushes to greet the returning prisoner of war in California in 1973.

The United States recently asked private American charities to give the Vietnamese assistance. They pointed out that 300,000 Vietnamese need artificial limbs and the training that goes along with such devices. America continues to prevent trade with the country except for so-called humanitarian aid. Privately, U.S. officials hope this roundabout way of helping the Vietnamese will result in more cooperation on the MIA front. Most people who study Indochina believe there are no living American soldiers left in Vietnam.

With the continuing discussion of MIAs, it's easy to forget those who were prisoners of war. A spokesman for the Veterans Administration says, "They went through a lot—as much as prisoners in any other war. They're heroes, which makes them different from earlier POWs. This is the first war where prisoners are heroes. People realize that it is not a dishonorable thing to be captured. In fact, living through it is heroic. These are my guys!" Most Vietnam-era POWs have returned to and been welcomed by American society.

Chapter 7

Refugees

Throughout its history, Vietnam has had large Chinese communities. These "overseas Chinese" became teachers, middle-class shopkeepers, skilled workers, and businessmen. During much of the Vietnam war, they continued their lives as usual, sending their sons and daughters out of the country to school and living quietly but well as the fighting raged all around them. These hard-working city dwellers were Vietnamese by birth but Chinese by language and culture. In Saigon, they had an entire section of town, named Cholon, to call their own. The suburb was ripped apart by terrible fighting during the 1968 Tet Offensive.

Chinese families worked hard all week, then each Sunday many drove their large foreign cars to the seaside resort of Vung Tau. They looked odd, dodging armored personnel carriers and bicycles as they headed north to Bien Hoa and east to the ocean. There were also thriving Chinese communities in Hué and Danang and in cities in North Vietnam.

This properous way of life was endangered when in 1975 the communists rolled into major cities in their Russian-made tanks. The Chinese wanted to continue their free trade businesses, but the conquering soldiers wanted to enroll all workers in cooperatives. The Vietnamese have never trusted the Chinese. The new Vietnamese government was unable for almost three years to end the free-enterprise system the Chinese operated.

In March 1978, the government organized groups of Vietnamese to search for shops and industries where private enterprise still existed. The Chinese owners were given little compensation for the machinery and equipment taken by the government. To make matters

Vietnamese refugees hurry ashore in South Vietnam during the war's final days. Civilian suffering throughout the war was intense.

worse, the Vietnamese secretly changed the kind of paper money being used. Some Chinese went to bed wealthy and awoke with worthless pieces of paper. Young Chinese were drafted and sent to fight without training on the front lines in Cambodia. Chinese—along with many Vietnamese who had not fled the country earlier—began to search for ways to leave Vietnam. The only method seemed to be by boat.

The Vietnamese government was desperate for money to run the country. To acquire cash, it charged each of the boat people—departing men, women or children—a high price to get aboard old, unsafe boats and be towed out into the South China Sea. So many people wanted to leave Vietnam that the rickety fishing boats were soon replaced by huge, rusted freighters and other large vessels. These battered ships, unfit for the sea, meant that refugees were still at great risk long after leaving Vietnam. At first, neighbors such as Hong Kong, Indonesia, Malaysia, the Philippines, and Thailand took in the refugees. Camps were set up until other nations could be found to welcome the boat people as new citizens.

For every refugee who landed safely, another was attacked by Malay or Thai pirates. Many refugees were robbed of their few possessions and raped or killed. Those with little or no money often had the worst tales of all to tell. They left Vietnam secretly by night in boats not meant for the open sea. The boats capsized, and most or all aboard were drowned. In other cases, these inexperienced "sailors" floated until they ran out of food and water. Those who died first were sometimes eaten by the others. To make matters worse, nearby countries began to turn away the refugees. Malaysia, with its large minority of Chinese, accepted 50,000 boat people and then closed its ports. The Malaysians pointed out that they had done their share and that the stability of their emerging nation was at stake. They did not have the industry or resources to absorb more new arrivals.

The 1.4 million Vietnamese and 300,000 Chinese from Vietnam weren't accepted automatically by anyone. Singapore took very few

South Vietnamese cling to inner tubes as they beg to be picked up by a Vietnamese navy ship off China Beach, Danang, in 1975.

of the refugees. The area's other major citystate, Hong Kong, allowed the boat people to anchor or to enter camps. Not until other countries accepted the refugees were they allowed out of the temporary camps. Considering the fact that Vietnam's neighbors were not wealthy, they did all they could. Even so, half of the boat people who left Vietnam died before touching land again. Some survived the terrible ocean trip only to drown as they tried to land on a wave-swept beach.

Conditions in the refugee camps grew worse in the 1980s. Thailand, with thousands of Laotian and Cambodian refugees, also took in 150,000 or more Vietnamese. Their camps along the Cambodian border were neither clean nor safe. Artillery from Vietnamese forces looking for Cambodian guerrillas made life in a camp precarious. A Vietnamese named Tri drew a diagram for a visitor to a Thai camp. He made a square within a square. The inner square was prison in Vietnam. The outer square was the camp. He pointed to the outer square. "This is where I am now; it is still a prison."

Slowly, the camps are closing. The Vietnamese have cut the flow of boat people to an unauthorized few. One of the most notorious camps, Pulau Bidong island off Malaysia, is down to 5,000 refugees from a high of 45,000. Approximately 850,000 refugees from Southeast Asia have come to the United States. Some 650,000 more have settled in Canada, France, and other Western countries. There are many more Cambodians, Laotians, and Vietnamese who would like to leave, but they are too old or poor or without families. Now that Cambodia, Laos, and Vietnam can produce enough food for their people, departures have dropped.

Refugees face many new problems. The Southeast Asians in the United States have had difficulty adjusting to life in America. A Hmong tribesman has said it was like being "on the moon." Primitive people such as the Hmong and other tribes have had an especially difficult ordeal. "We can't get used to the familiarity between men and women," said a Hmong ex-soldier. "We are not used to people you hardly know acting as if they are your friends.

Vietnamese depart a ship that has run aground near the harbor of Hong Kong. These refugees fled Vietnam in 1979.

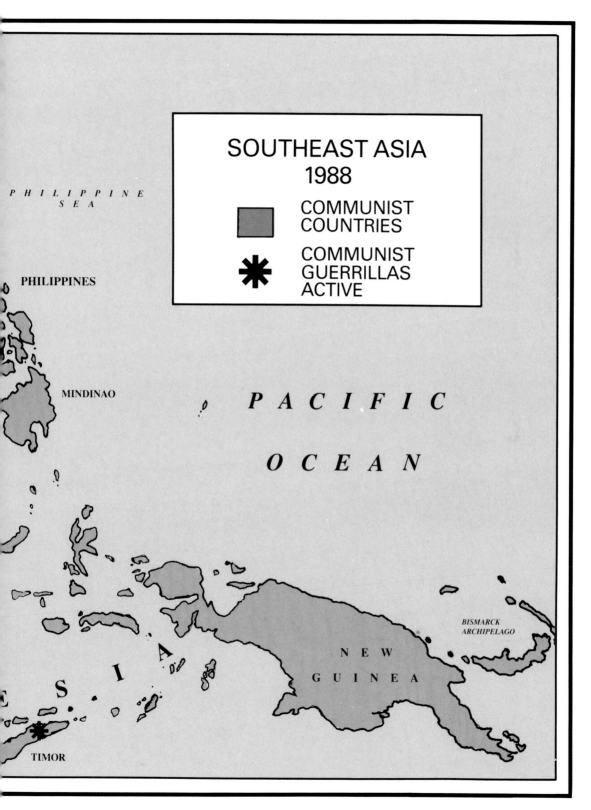

**SOUTHEAST ASIA
1988**

COMMUNIST
COUNTRIES

COMMUNIST
GUERRILLAS
ACTIVE

*PHILIPPINE
SEA*

PHILIPPINES

MINDINAO

P A C I F I C

O C E A N

*BISMARCK
ARCHIPELAGO*

E S I A

N E W
G U I N E A

TIMOR

Two Vietnamese women haggle over the price of fish in New Orleans. Some 4,000 Vietnamese have settled in the Louisiana city, one of many coastal cities with active Vietnamese communities.

And we are concerned about helping our own people. If the Hmong do not help their people, nobody will.'' Children seem to adjust better than adults, in part because they learn English in school. Middle-aged refugees are easily depressed. They are unable to support themselves and feel ashamed that they are on welfare.

California, with its huge oriental population, has the majority of Vietnamese new to this country. In Los Angeles, Seattle, and elsewhere there are young Southeast Asians, barely past high school age, who join gangs. They are Vietnamese and Chinese who have not learned English well and were older than their fellow students. They have turned to lives of gambling, drinking, drugs, and crime. A young Chinese man from Saigon shot and killed a Los Angeles police officer who walked in on a Chinatown jewelry store robbery in 1984. Different kinds of problems take place at home. The American Refugee Committee says there is "growing evidence of mental health problems in the refugee population" of many big cities. Chemical dependency, family violence, and suicide are all on the increase among these Asian people.

Even when refugees find work, difficulties may not end. Because Vietnamese fishermen don't understand how the American fishing industry works, those living on the Texas and Louisiana Gulf Coast have clashed with local residents. Hundreds of Vietnamese, ignorant of laws and regulations, overfished shrimp beds. They fouled the nets of American fishermen. The locals reacted by shooting at some of the new citizens and holding Ku Klux

Tung Dang, a refugee in 1980, learned English, graduated from high school and college with honors, and now holds an important job with a major U.S. company. He is just 20 years old.

Klan rallies. Most of the Vietnamese remained, though some migrated eastward to Biloxi, Mississippi. There, many women have found work in seafood-processing plants. Wherever the Southeast Asians arrive, there are new problems and new opportunities.

On the positive side, their children's success in U.S. schools has caused amazement. Many Southeast Asian children do better in American schools than do children who were born in the U.S. Educators believe Asian Americans value education more. Surveys show that they study longer and harder. They also look at school differently—they know that doing well in school means success as an adult. Behind each star student is a family who wants what many members will never have: a fresh start in a new country as a young man or woman. Parents who were professionals in their native country now work long hours in low-paying jobs so that their sons and daughters can learn. Children feel they will fulfill the dreams of their mothers and fathers.

Some Asian American adults have been highly successful. Yen Do is publisher of *Nguoi Viet*, the free world's only daily newspaper in the Vietnamese language. He came to California in 1975 with a good education and with his immediate family but little else. He recalls that starting the newspaper was a tremendous task. Type was set in the normal alphabet. Then, 8,000 accent marks were drawn by hand every day for seven years! The newspaper now has a computer that typesets the heavily accented Vietnamese language. Yen Do also produces television shows in his native language from the community room that is part of the newspaper building. Although he is a success, he cannot forget about his mother and sister who remain in Vietnam. Yen Do receives about four letters a year and sends them gifts. But, he says, it is dangerous for them to be in contact with him.

Speaking of danger, one tiny minority has lived a perilous existence in Vietnam since America left. They are children whose mothers are Vietnamese and whose fathers are Americans. When the French left Vietnam,

A Vietnamese girl studies English in Florida. Many refugees were given short courses in "survival English" after their arrival in the United States.

they took with them all their
Eurasian children and all mothers
of Eurasians who wished to leave.
Today there are about 15,000
young Amerasian adults in Vietnam. These are people whose
fathers are Americans. The U.S.
has managed to bring only 4,000
to America. Not many know their
fathers. They suffer discrimination by the Vietnamese, who do
not seem to care if they live or die.
Fortunately, an agreement made
between the U.S. and Vietnam
early in 1988 allows 400 people a
week to leave Vietnam. Some
Amerasian children surely will be
on these flights from Ho Chi
Minh City (formerly Saigon) to
Bangkok.

Success stories like Yen Do's
will increase as Southeast Asians
learn how their new country
works. For the first generation,
however, success usually comes
hard. One third of all Vietnamese
now living in America have
incomes below the poverty line.
Three of every four Hmong are
on some sort of public assistance.
Yet, like other minorities who
began in poverty, this latest wave
of immigrants can also work their
way to success.

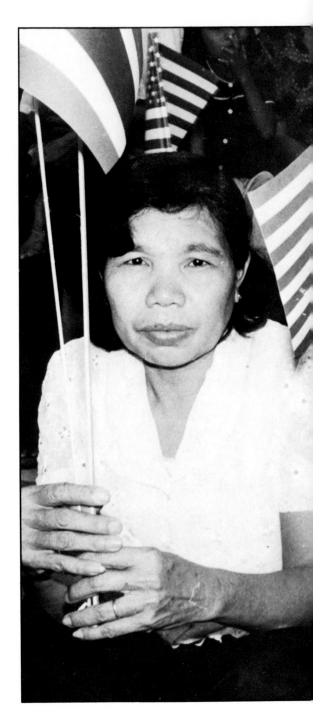

Vietnamese fly the U.S. flag at a refugee camp in Thailand in 1978. Sadly, some refugees remain in camps and have little chance of gaining citizenship anywhere.

Chapter 8

Vietnam After the War

Once the war was over, the South Vietnamese discovered quickly that northerners were good at war but poor at peace. In villages and hamlets throughout the South, Viet Cong members took over local governments; but the North Vietnamese Army made and enforced the rules. A former Viet Cong reported subtle but very real discrimination toward southerners. They had few of the powerful positions in the new national government. Known to be more relaxed than northerners, the South Vietnamese tried to adapt to military rules.

Life under the NVA proved to be drab and strict. In Saigon, 100 tons of books were seized in one year and Western music was banned. All coffee houses, bars, and night clubs were closed. A man in Can Tho entertained his friends by showing them a horror movie one evening. He was caught, and officials sentenced him to a prison term. "There are tin-horn dictators everywhere," one worker said, "and living under them isn't fun."

High-ranking members of the South Vietnamese government fled the country in 1975. Low-ranking members were ignored. Those in between were sent off to re-education camps. These were supposed to be pleasant places where capitalists spent a few months being educated to become communists.

Since the country was united in 1975, however, an estimated 40,000 men and women still remain in the camps, which are really rural prisons. People are made to work long hours under armed guards, with little food and only the barest necessities. Catholic priests, Buddhist monks, and other religious leaders have been sent to the camps, where some stubborn "students" have been killed.

Life is regimented and very hard in today's Vietnam.

More than 1.5 million ordinary citizens have been moved to "new economic zones." These are areas not well suited for farming. Yet farms are needed to feed the population, which now numbers 60 million. There is enough food to eat but no surplus. Rice has been rationed since the fall of Saigon.

When the U.S. ambassador left, he took with him a huge aid package. Suddenly, the Vietnamese were without the cushion of U.S. aid they had enjoyed for years. There were no longer imports of rice or other grains, no clothing, no medicine, and little to sell on the black market. "Everybody was skinny," says a member of the American Friends Service Committee, which has provided civilians with tools and medicine for many years. His and other volunteer services, such as World Vision and England's Oxfam, no longer operated in the country. As late as 1982, the government said all children were malnourished. Quality medicine was so scarce that there was a massive return to ancient Chinese healing practices. The Vietnamese turned to whoever would lend them food or money, agricultural experts, or technicians. Russia and several Asian neighbors responded, even though the Vietnamese could not guarantee any sort of repayment schedule. In fact, they failed to repay a loan from the Japanese that was due in 1982.

Persons who thought reuniting the country would bring peace were wrong. The Vietnamese and the Chinese were once described as being "as close as lips and teeth." Now, they snarl at each other across the border north of Hanoi. In the Mekong Delta after 1975, members of the Khmer Rouge (Cambodian communists) attacked innocent villages, killing dozens of farmers and their families. On December 25, 1978, the Vietnamese army launched several successful attacks into Cambodia. Pol Pot was forced to leave Phnom Penh and flee into the western hills near Thailand.

Vietnam's sudden move into Cambodia made China decide to punish the Vietnamese for their aggression. The breakdown of Vietnamese-Chinese relations did not happen overnight. For years, the two countries had clashed along the border they share.

Refugee camps never empty, in part because the U.S. has refused to recognize the present Vietnamese government and establish diplomatic relations.

China became an ally of the Pol Pot regime in part because it feared the military success of the Vietnamese. In 1979 thousands of Chinese crossed into Vietnam amid heavy artillery and automatic weapons fire. The Vietnamese fought well but soon retreated, badly outnumbered by the Chinese. China, having proved its point, gave a final warning to Vietnam and called its troops home. In both campaigns, hundreds of Vietnamese troops died. To this day, thousands of Vietnamese soldiers still remain on guard in Cambodia and thousands more are on alert where China invaded in 1979.

Not all of the problems have come from outside Vietnam. As many as 20,000 anticommunist guerrillas were active in the country as late as 1982. They may be supported by the Chinese—or by the U.S. The Montagnard minority, who never liked the Vietnamese, continue to cling stubbornly to their traditions. With some provinces only 15 percent Vietnamese, problems are likely. In 1982, several highlands tribes staged a long rebellion.

That same year, two Viet-

Khmer Rouge Cambodians were driven into the western hills by attacking Vietnamese.

Cambodia has no money and few skilled people to make repairs following years of war.

namese stole a boat and tried to leave the country with their families. They were caught by the shore patrol. One of the organizers of the escape was put to death and the other sentenced to 20 years in prison.

Corruption in the new government may be as bad as it was in the old. The government spends a lot of time trying to stop people who deal illegally in gold, jewelry, opium, and other goods. They reported in 1983 that 17 percent of all fertilizer is stolen and sold privately.

The new leaders are also undecided about how to handle the issue of freedom of religion. At first, people were told to fly Buddhist flags if they had no flags representing the Viet Cong. Since then, relations between the government and religious groups have been strained. The communist leaders believe all four million Roman Catholics are secretly pro-Western; perhaps they are. The Buddhists are activists who demand their rights in a land where the government decides which rights to grant. And members of such sects as the Cao Dai simply don't want rules imposed on their religion. In 1983, two Cao Dai members were killed and 33 imprisoned for antigovernment activity. Later that same year, a 14-year-old boy was killed by a policeman's bayonet during a religious demonstration. In 1984, Buddhist leader Thich Tri Thu died, probably in jail. To keep an eye on protestors, the government has tried to form its own religious associations for Catholics and Buddhists. However, few people have joined these associations.

With the world's third largest army, Vietnam's soldiers and veterans present problems for the administration. There are half a million disabled veterans, young and old. Casualties still occur in Cambodia. There are many veterans still alive who fought the French 34 years ago. Disabled and healthy veterans alike have a hard time finding jobs. They are respected, but there simply are

The black market continues openly in Ho Chi Minh City, formerly Saigon, as this 1985 photo shows. Despite food shortages, there are plenty of radios, TV sets, and other products.

not many jobs available. Big cities are filled with disabled people who ask for money on the streets. One news service reported that a large group of these veterans staged a protest recently over lack of artificial limbs, hearing aids, and glasses. With many able-bodied people out of work, the veterans have a long wait for employment or other benefits.

Problems have been so numerous that the government has lost popular support. Aging leaders resigned or were fired late in 1986 and were replaced by younger, less strict men. These new leaders say they are less interested in policies and more interested in creating jobs, improving harvests, and upgrading the country in general. Small private enterprises, such as restaurants and bicycle shops, can now operate openly, competing for customers.

It will take more than private enterprise, however, to overcome rising prices, crop failures, counterfeiting, corruption, incompetence, and lack of skills. Social problems, unknown before the war, are now common. Juvenile delinquents are everywhere; students now disobey or even attack teachers. An underground economy sells such rationed goods as meat, sugar, soap, rice, and gasoline. Vietnam's new rulers have tough jobs ahead of them.

With this in mind, what is Vietnam like for today's typical citizen? He or she is likely to live in the countryside, since 80 percent of Vietnam is rural. Work probably consists of tending rice, which is either planted, cared for, or harvested the year round. There's a weekly trip to the market. Fruits, vegetables, pork, fish, spices, and other items are sold. Returning home, the resident lives in a thatched hut with two or three rooms. There is no electricity, but there may be a small portable radio. Entertainment at night used to be only political lectures. Now, that has decreased, and the people are happier without these long, dull meetings. There is plenty to do to keep alive and well, in contrast to Vietnam's cities. There, thousands of usually ambitious Vietnamese are unemployed or have only part-time jobs. Unlike a developed country, Vietnam's rural areas are more active than are its cities.

Reminders of the war can be found in city and countryside alike. Not many of the damaged buildings in Ho Chi Minh City have been repaired, though construction always seems to be under way. Northern areas, such as Haiphong, were hammered repeatedly in bombing raids. These places still are filled with rubble. Rusted U.S. trucks, tanks, strips of metal used for runways, and corrugated containers lie in fields and ditches. The weapons are gone, collected by the government. Yet in rural areas mines and unexploded bombs remain hidden and sometimes kill or injure farmers who accidentally strike them with plows or step on them. Huge areas of forest stand naked, their leaves and plants destroyed by Agent Orange. It will be 100 years before growth begins again. Amazingly, dozens of temples and monasteries are still in one piece, and some of the most scenic beaches and mountain

Hanoi residents crowd a state store for sugar. Most food items are strictly rationed, though individuals often sell garden vegetables and other crops they raise.

This Vietnamese now owns a small piece of land but growing rice remains hard work.

areas show no scars from the fighting. Just as important, the people are friendly.

These and other attractions have created a tourist industry for the country, which badly needs foreign money. Perhaps the presence of foreigners will make the leaders a bit less suspicious. At the moment, some of them still believe that the United States and China meet to think of ways to keep Vietnam poor and backward. The Vietnamese do not trust other neighbors, such as Thailand. They have shelled Thai villages near the Cambodian border and attacked Thai patrols. When China withdrew its support of Thailand's tiny band of communist guerrillas, Vietnam began to supply these guerrillas with weapons. It is probably the intent of the Vietnamese to keep Cambodia and Laos even poorer and more undeveloped than Vietnam so they cannot pose a threat to the newly reunited country. While Vietnam, Cambodia, and Laos continue to struggle economically, other Southeast Asian nations are doing well. These nations could serve as models for Vietnam's new leaders.

Chapter 9

Many Questions, Few Answers

There have been longer wars, bloodier wars, and wars begun by mistake. But there has never been a war that left so many questions with so few answers. Vietnam is not pleasant to think about. Neither are the lingering questions. . .

Q: Why did we decide to help the South Vietnamese?

A: The United States after World War II believed that its job was to stop the spread of communism. No matter where communism was growing, the U.S. believed it should be stamped out. The "domino theory" was part of our belief. According to this theory, if communists take over one country, they will take over the next and the next and the next— just like dominoes knocking each other down. Was this theory proved true by the fall of Laos and Cambodia? Or do the health of Thailand and Malaysia prove it false? Did American involvement in Vietnam buy time for nearby nations to develop? It may be impossible to tell. One thing has changed, however. Not many Americans today think we should be global policemen.

Q: Which U.S. President got us into Vietnam?

A: Each President since World War II made commitments that later Presidents were forced to honor. The first major mistake may have been made by the Truman administration. Ho Chi Minh admired Americans and in 1945 turned to them for help in creating an independent Vietnam. The U.S. had been an ally of the French during the war and did not take sides when the French returned. From that point on, relations with the North Vietnamese grew steadily worse.

Veterans still search for answers about Vietnam.

Q: How could so much killing of innocent civilians take place?

A: This question is asked after all wars because there are always innocent casualties. For example, a character in a Woody Allen movie is asked how the Germans could have wiped out millions in World War II concentration camps. "You're asking me why there are Nazis? I don't even know how the can opener works." That's not as silly an answer as it seems. The character is saying that killing innocent people is such a huge question that he doesn't even know how to approach it. That can be said in particular of Cambodia, where communists seemed to take pleasure in torturing and killing their own people. From the few photos and eyewitness accounts, Khmer Rouge members never worked alone. Just as on a battlefield, being in a group may have given these Cambodians the courage to commit acts they might not have done alone.

Both sides in Vietnam killed civilians. Americans killed them most often by accident in artillery strikes or bombing raids. But My Lai 4 could not be blamed on a

bomb. Nor could the Phoenix program, which resulted in the deaths of civilians merely suspected of aiding the Viet Cong. NVA and VC killing was seen on an awful scale in Hué during the Tet Offensive. The South Vietnamese on their part routinely tortured and killed their prisoners. On the other hand, most soldiers fighting in the war did not commit any atrocities.

Members of Vietnam Veterans Against the War (VVAW) hold a mock raid on the steps of the U.S. Capital in 1971. VVAW actions caused soldiers and civilians to examine their feelings about the war.

A related question that could be asked is: Why do we have so little regard for our fellow humans that we fight wars over and over? Again, we have no sure answer for this question either.

Q: How did the war affect the United States?

A: There are more answers to this question than there are grains of rice in a bowl. Here is a short list:

• Millions of American citizens no longer believe everything their government tells them. One of the major casualties of the war was the truth, which government officials bent and twisted to suit their plans. Citizens became aware of this and feel today that bending and twisting the truth occurs often in many governmental areas.

• The U.S. public today is very

Kent State University students in Ohio flee tear gas during a 1970 demonstration. A few moments later, National Guardsmen fired into a crowd of students, killing four and wounding several others.

skeptical about getting involved in Central America, where Nicaragua has a communist government. Food and nonmilitary supplies have been shipped to rebels, but no American troops have been sent. "Brushfire" wars such as the one in Central America are dangerous, and the U.S. is no longer the free world's policeman.

• America has become more conservative since Vietnam. In the 1970s conservatives blamed liberals, pacifists, educators— even clergymen—for the fall of South Vietnam. President Reagan was elected in 1980 in part because he promised to confront communism and restore respectability to defense.

• The military is held in disregard by many veterans. The armed forces were respected by the public at the start of the war. As the fighting dragged on that opinion deteriorated—and so did the military. This was because of dwindling public support at home, and the disillusionment of many soldiers with the country's role in Vietnam. The elimination of the draft created a whole different set of questions about the nature and role of the armed forces in United States policy.

• Historians look at Vietnam as marking the end of what is known as the American century, during which the U.S. emerged as a world power. The "century" began in 1898, during the administration of Theodore Roosevelt, whose motto was "Speak softly and carry a big stick." The country gained strength in World War I, when U.S. troops helped stop the German advance in France. U.S.

Protesters taunt National Guardsmen during the 1968 Democratic convention in Chicago.

power reached a new peak at the end of World War II. Europe lay in ruins, while the U.S. had built a tremendous industrial base. The U.S. also had invented the atomic bomb, the most powerful weapon ever devised.

But Americans proved to be human when the Korean War ended in a toss-up. They proved human when they allowed the Japanese, who had staged a miraculous comeback, to gain world economic leadership. They proved human as they lay dying in Vietnam, burdened by heavy weapons and poor leadership against a ghostlike enemy. Some feel the American century may have ended in 1974, when Middle East oil kingdoms created a new center of power. Or, it may have come to a close on April 30, 1975, the day North Vietnamese soldiers swept into Saigon. Others feel the American century is still alive, only going through profound changes as other countries emerge as leaders.

Q: Why were the South Vietnamese unable to defend themselves?

A: Let's ask a former South Vietnamese, publisher Yen Do, whom we met earlier. He says, "The South saw America intervene beginning in 1962 and 1963. They thought this American insurance would never end. The North Vietnamese had to fight because there was no one to fight for them."

Other views include the fact that the South had no military tradition. Some NVA and Viet Cong officers were veterans of fighting against the French. They had beaten a Western power in 1954 and believed they could do so again. Older officers in the Army of the Republic of Vietnam (ARVN) fought for the French but never took part in major decisions. When American advisers arrived in the early 1960s, they found the best South Vietnamese units close to Saigon, guarding the country's capital.

The U.S. helped train thousands of South Vietnamese, but many young soldiers did not have their minds on a military life. They saw opportunities to make money serving the needs and amusements of U.S. personnel. Also, South Vietnamese soldiers were fighting nearer their homes than were the NVA troops. Many

Many South Vietnamese cared little about politics and simply wanted to survive the war.

of them were followed into battle by their families. If a soldier's family was near a battlefield, the soldier was likely to visit them without permission or to desert altogether. The rapid fall of the central highlands in 1975 was partly due to hundreds of South Vietnamese troops leaving to search for and take care of their parents, wives, and children.

Q: Why were U.S. soldiers unable to beat the North Vietnamese and the Viet Cong?

In the strict sense of the words, U.S. soldiers beat the enemy badly in every major battle. Vastly superior American firepower and mobility forced the communists to continue a war of ambushes, boobytraps, and other hit-and-run tactics. NVA and Viet Cong members also were skilled at hiding in elaborate tunnel complexes, swamps, and caves and in blending with the local population.

American soldiers did not know why they were in Vietnam. They were told to win the "hearts and minds" of the Vietnamese people. Yet they quickly saw that many Vietnamese did not like Americans and that the natives were too busy trying to survive to care who ran the country. In contrast, the enemy's goal was to unify all Vietnamese. To do this, they had to drive out the U.S. and other foreign troops.

Overwhelming air power influenced the war but could not win it. North Vietnam produced little in the way of industry or manufactured goods. It was only a receiving point for weapons and supplies sent by other countries. After the first few months, there were no factories left to bomb. Continuous bombing of civilians, North or South, only drove more and more people to support the NVA or VC.

U.S. soldiers were young. The average man in the field was 19 years old, compared to 27 for the average American soldier in World War II. The military did not know how to handle such young soldiers and did a bad job. Many experienced officers lost faith in their superiors and left the military, while new officers were inexperienced or incompetent. Career officers wanted to be in combat briefly so their personnel files would list combat experience. How could young men learn anything when their officers were being moved in and out of the fighting? How could they believe in officers who won awards without being near the battle? Awards became so nonsensical in the Army that some enlisted men got a medal of bravery awarded to their dog!

Drugs also played a part. Some units had many heavy drug users while other soldiers did not even smoke marijuana. Alcohol was available and was sold inexpensively by the military to its soldiers. At Camp Bearcat, 9th Infantry Division soldiers paid 15 cents for a can of soda, but only 10 cents for a can of beer. Drinking was an approved form of drug abuse. None of the drugs improved a situation that got worse as time went on.

No single factor caused the South to fall. Rather, it was hundreds of little things. For example. . . Russian ships were anchored near Pacific island runways to warn the North Vietnamese of B-52 bombers taking off. . . . There were an estimated 30,000 spies in the South Vietnamese government, but none among the NVA. . . . The enemy spoke Vietnamese and the U.S.

Not even superior firepower can win an unpopular war.

forces aiding South Vietnam did not. . . . Some of the most complex tunnels were built under American bases, such as the ones found beneath the U.S. 25th Infantry Division base camp at Cu Chi. . . . The list of enemy advantages was large indeed.

Q: How can we avoid future Vietnams?

A: That may be the most important question of all. The Soviet Union recently was involved in a war in Afghanistan that was similar to Vietnam. The Soviets backed an unpopular government.

Their enemies were furnished aid and modern weapons by other countries. And the Russians were fighting people who moved freely across borders. You would think that the Soviets might have learned from the U.S. experience in Southeast Asia, but such was not the case. It remains to be seen whether America has learned from its own experience or will allow itself to become involved in a shooting war elsewhere such as in Central America. While the recent treaty to curb U.S. and Soviet warheads may help prevent nuclear war, it will do little to stop conventional clashes. Nations must be more willing to use diplomatic skills to solve problems.

On an individual basis, every person must decide what is best for him or her in a troubled time. If many believe their country's involvement in a war is right, they will fight and probably win. If people feel a war is morally wrong, their protests may help prevent or end the war. Not until most people on both sides prefer to talk, or refuse to bear arms, will wars be a thing of the past.

Vietnamese learn English following their arrival in the United States. Vietnamese and native Americans want the Vietnamese here to succeed while maintaining important parts of their culture.

In Recognition of the Women in Vietnam

About 10,000 American women were in Vietnam as soldiers or civilians during the period 1964-1975. The majority were in the military, and 90 percent of all military women were nurses. Eight military women died while in Vietnam. Their names are carved into the Vietnam Veterans Memorial in Washington, D.C. There is no accurate record of how many Vietnamese women lost their lives during this period.

Five of the eight servicewomen died when planes or helicopters in which they were riding crashed. One woman died in a rocket attack. Two other deaths were attributed to medical reasons— one succumbed to a stroke and the other died of complications caused by pneumonia. Of the eight, an Air Force nurse died in the crash of the C-5A Galaxy aircraft that lost a door shortly after takeoff from Saigon's Tan Son Nhut Air Base on April 8, 1975. Her death was one of 172 in the tragedy; most persons on the plane were Vietnamese children.

The Red Cross provided 480 field workers, many of them women. They worked among the wounded in hospitals and made sure that messages between soldiers and their families were sent and received. A total of 322 clubmobile workers, young college graduate women, were sent by the Red Cross to Vietnam at the request of the military. They visited isolated base camps during duty hours. Their assignment was to make life a little more bearable for combat soldiers. Three of these Red Cross women died in Vietnam. One was killed when her Jeep overturned, one died of disease, and one was murdered as she slept. Her murder was never solved.

The number of American women involved in Vietnam is small compared to the number of Vietnamese women. The Viet Cong, like the U.S., depended on women in noncombat roles. However, Viet Cong women and civilians alike often found the war thrust upon them. It is a tribute to these women that they kept their sanity as the war killed friends and relatives, destroyed their homes, and brought them repeatedly into the line of fire in a war with no front lines.

After years of effort to gain recognition, it appears that the

About 10,000 American women served in Vietnam.

women who served in the U.S. military will have their share of attention. The Vietnam Women's Memorial Project has been given approval to erect a statue of a woman in Vietnam-era fatigue uniform. The statue is to share the 2.2 acres in Washington, D.C. set aside for the wall and the statue of the three male soldiers. Like the male soldiers, this statue would face the V-shaped wall of names.

Timeline of Vietnam: 3000 B.C. to 1988

3000 B.C. The people we call the Vietnamese begin to migrate south out of China.

100 B.C. Start of China's 1,000-year rule of Vietnam.

A.D. 938 Vietnam becomes independent.

1500 The first European explorers visit Vietnam.

1640 Alexandre de Rhodes, a French Roman Catholic missionary, arrives in Vietnam.

1744 Vietnam expands into the Mekong Delta. The Vietnamese by this date rule over all of present-day Vietnam.

1844 The French fleet destroys Vietnam's navy.

1859 Saigon falls to the French.

1883 The French capture Hanoi.

1930 Ho Chi Minh starts the Indochinese Communist Party.

1939 The communist party is outlawed in Vietnam.

1941 The Japanese take control of Vietnam as Ho Chi Minh returns from a Chinese prison and the Viet Minh (communist army) is founded.

1945 Ho Chi Minh declares Vietnam independent as the Japanese surrender.

1946 The French return, and the Viet Minh take to the hills as the French Indochina war begins.

1952 Viet Minh forces are defeated several times by the French.

1954 The French are defeated at Dien Bien Phu and agree to leave Vietnam. Vietnam is divided into north and south following a cease-fire agreed upon in Geneva, Switzerland.

1955 The U.S. begins to send aid to South Vietnam.

1956 President Ngo Dinh Diem refuses to hold elections, as had been promised in the Geneva agreement.

1957 Communist guerrilla activities begin in South Vietnam.

1959 The North Vietnamese start to send soldiers into South Vietnam.

1963 The Viet Cong (South Vietnamese communists) defeat regular South Vietnamese soldiers at Ap Bac. This is the first major battle between the two sides. Buddhists protest South Vietnamese government policies. President Diem is overthrown and killed by the military.

1964 A North Vietnamese patrol boat attacks an American destroyer in the Gulf of Tonkin. Congress gives President Lyndon B. Johnson special powers to act in Southeast Asia. The first American pilot is shot down and taken prisoner by the North Vietnamese.

1965

1965 American air raids take place over North Vietnam. The first American combat troops arrive in South Vietnam.

February 7 Viet Cong attack U.S. bases. President Johnson replies to the attacks by bombing targets in North Vietnam.

March 8 The first American combat soldiers—3,500 Marines—arrive in Vietnam to guard Danang airbase.

March 24 Antiwar teach-in is held at the University of Michigan, Ann Arbor, Michigan. Teach-ins take place throughout 1965 on many college and university campuses.

April North Vietnamese prepare the first launching pad for Russian surface-to-air (SAM) missiles.

May 15 National antiwar teach-in held in Washington, D.C.

May 24 First U.S. Army division leaves U.S. for Vietnam.

June 11 Air Force General Nguyen Cao Ky takes over as South Vietnam's prime minister.

July 28 General William Westmoreland, commander of American forces in Vietnam, asks for and gets an increase in U.S. troops.

October through mid-November U.S. Army soldiers defeat North Vietnamese Army (NVA) troops in the first major battle between American and North Vietnamese forces. The fighting takes place in the remote Ia Drang valley.

December 25 U.S. bombing of North Vietnam is suspended by President Lyndon B. Johnson, who hopes the North Vietnamese will meet with him to talk peace.

December 31 U.S. troop strength in Vietnam numbers 200,000.

1966

January 31 President Johnson orders the bombing of North Vietnam to resume.

January-February The Senate Foreign Relations Committee questions President Johnson's advisers about U.S. involvement in the war.

February 8 President Johnson and South Vietnamese leaders call for peace following a meeting in Hawaii.

March 10 Buddhists demonstrate against the South Vietnamese government. Ky responds by using troops to quell demonstrations.

April 12 B-52 bombers are used for the first time in bombing raids against North Vietnam.

December North Vietnamese leaders meet and agree to fight the war with both troops and diplomacy.

1967

January North Vietnam says that the U.S. must stop its air raids before peace talks can begin.

January Operation Cedar Falls begins. This massive military action is designed to rid the Iron Triangle near Saigon of enemy soldiers. Villages believed sympathetic to the Viet Cong are levelled and the people relocated to refugee camps.

February 22 Operation Junction City begins. A plan to trap Viet Cong in a jungle area northwest of Saigon, the operation results in few VC captured despite five major battles.

April 28 General William Westmoreland addresses Congress on the war in Vietnam, asking for greater support.

July The North Vietnamese meet to plan a "Great Uprising" in 1968 in the south. The uprising became known as the Tet Offensive.

August Secretary of Defense Robert McNamara meets behind closed doors with U.S. senators. He informs them the saturation bombing of North Vietnam is not weakening the North Vietnamese.

September 3 General Nguyen Van Thieu is elected president of South Vietnam.

November U.S. Marines occupy Khe Sanh, a hilltop near the border of Laos. They are soon surrounded by over 35,000 NVA soldiers.

December 31 The number of U.S. troops in Vietnam reaches nearly 500,000.

1968

January 30-31 The Tet Offensive begins as Viet Cong and North Vietnamese troops attack most of the major cities in South Vietnam and the major American military bases.

February 24 U.S. and South Vietnamese forces, after weeks of fighting, retake Hué, ending the Tet Offensive.

March 10 *The New York Times* reports that General William Westmoreland wants 206,000 more American troops by the end of the year.

March 12 Eugene McCarthy, the antiwar U.S. senator from Minnesota, receives 40 percent of the Democratic vote in the New Hampshire primary.

March 16 Between 200 and 600 Vietnamese civilians are murdered by American troops in a village called My Lai 4.

March 31 President Lyndon B. Johnson orders a halt to the bombing of North Vietnam and announces that he will not run again for the presidency.

April 4 Dr. Martin Luther King, Jr., is shot to death in Memphis, Tennessee. Rioting erupts in many large U.S. cities.

May 11 Formal peace talks begin in Paris between the United States and North Vietnam.

June 6 U.S. Senator Robert Kennedy dies the day after he is shot in Los Angeles, California. Kennedy had been campaigning for the Democratic Presidential nomination.

June 10 General Creighton Abrams takes command of U.S. forces in Vietnam.

June 27 American troops leave Khe Sanh after several months of bitter fighting.

July 1 U.S. planes resume bombing north of the DMZ.

August 8 Richard M. Nixon is nominated by Republicans to run for the presidency.

August 26-29 Vice President Hubert Humphrey is nominated for the presidency in Chicago as police and antiwar demonstrators clash violently in the city's streets.

November 6 Richard M. Nixon is elected President.

December 31 A total of 540,000 Americans are in Vietnam.

1969

March 18 The secret bombing of Cambodia begins.

March 28 U.S. and ARVN troops discover mass graves of civilians killed by Viet Cong and NVA during the Tet takeover of Hué.

June 8 President Nixon announces that 25,000 American troops will be withdrawn, to be replaced by South Vietnamese forces.

September 3 Ho Chi Minh dies in Hanoi at the age of 79.

Fall Huge antiwar rallies take place in Washington, D.C.

November 16 The country learns of the My Lai 4 massacre.

December 31 The number of U.S. troops in South Vietnam drops to 480,000.

1970

February 20 Henry Kissinger and Le Duc Tho of North Vietnam meet secretly in Paris.

March 18 Prince Sihanouk of Cambodia is overthrown.

April 30 American and South Vietnamese forces invade Cambodia.

May 4 National Guardsmen kill 4 antiwar students and wound 11 others at Kent State University in Ohio.

December 31 The number of U.S. troops in Vietnam falls to 280,000.

1971

January 6 Congress repeals the Gulf of Tonkin Resolution.

February 8 South Vietnamese forces enter Laos in an attempt to cut the Ho Chi Minh trail.

March 29 Lieutenant William Calley is convicted of murder in connection with the massacre at My Lai 4.

December 31 U.S. forces now total 140,000.

1972

May 8 President Nixon orders the mining of Haiphong harbor and steps up the bombing.

June 17 A night watchman catches five men attempting to break into Democratic national headquarters at the Watergate apartment-hotel complex in Washington, D.C.

November 7 Richard Nixon is re-elected President.

December 31 U.S. combat troops number fewer than 30,000.

1973

January 27 An agreement is reached between the United States and North Vietnam to end the war in South Vietnam.

March 29 The last U.S. troops leave South Vietnam. The only Americans left behind are 8,500 civilians, plus embassy guards and a small number of soldiers in a defense office.

April 5 The U.S. Senate votes 88-3 to forbid aid to Vietnam without congressional approval.

August 15 The bombing of Cambodia by American planes ends. President Nixon criticizes Congress for ending the air war.

October 16 Henry Kissinger and Le Duc Tho are awarded the Nobel Peace Prize for ending the war in Indochina. Tho turns down the award because, as he points out, fighting continues.

1974

April 4 The U.S. House of Representatives rejects a White House proposal for more aid to South Vietnam.

August 9 Richard M. Nixon resigns as President of the United States and thus stops impeachment proceedings. Vice President Gerald Ford is sworn in as President.

1975

January 6 The province of Phuoc Long, only 60 miles north of Saigon, is captured by the communists.

March 14 President Nguyen Van Thieu decides to pull his troops out of the central highlands and northern provinces.

April 8 A huge U.S. cargo plane, loaded with Vietnamese orphans, crashes on takeoff near Saigon. More than 100 children die.

April 17 Cambodia falls to the Khmer Rouge (Cambodian communists).

April 30 Saigon falls to the communists.

December 3 Laos falls to the Pathet Lao (Laotian communists).

1976

July 2 The two Vietnams are officially reunified.

November 2 James Earl (Jimmy) Carter is elected President of the United States.

1977

January 21 President Carter pardons 10,000 draft evaders. Throughout the year more and more refugees ("boat people") leave Vietnam by any means available. Many are ethnic Chinese who fear persecution from Vietnamese victors.

1978

December Vietnamese forces occupy Cambodia.

1979

February 17 China invades Vietnam and is in the country for three weeks.

November 24 The U.S. General Accounting Office indicates that thousands of Vietnam veterans were exposed to the herbicide known as Agent Orange. The veterans claim they have suffered physical and psychological damage from the exposure.

1980

Summer Vietnamese army pursues Cambodians into Thailand.

November 4 Ronald Reagan is
elected President of the United
States.

1982

November 13 The Vietnam
Veterans' Memorial is
dedicated in Washington, D.C.

1984

May 7 Seven U.S. chemical
companies agree to an out-of-
court settlement with Vietnam
veterans over manufacture of
the herbicide Agent Orange.
The settlement is for $180
million.

July 15 Major fighting breaks out
along the Vietnam-China
border.

1986

December Vietnam's aging
leaders step down after failing
to improve the economy.

1988

June Vietnamese troops begin to
withdraw from Cambodia.

A Vietnamese woman sells French-
style hard rolls in Saigon during the
Tet Offensive in 1968.

Glossary

The glossary of each book in this series introduces various Vietnamese and American terms used throughout the war.

Democratic Kampuchea: The name given to Cambodia after its takeover by the communist Khmer Rouge in 1975.

Flashback: A sudden, vivid recall of a forgotten event. As it applies to a Vietnam veteran, it often means he remembers a very unpleasant moment. Some veterans say they have no control over such experiences.

Ho Chi Minh City: The name given Saigon after the Vietnamese communist takeover in 1975.

MIA: Missing in action. Said of soldiers who disappear in battle or while serving their country.

Pathet Lao: Laotian communists, backed by the North Vietnamese. They took control of Laos in 1975.

Post-traumatic stress: The feeling of fear, dread, etc., caused by an event that may have happened years ago. Vietnam veterans with mental problems feel these problems are caused by a battlefield trauma (shock) they suddenly remember. Flashbacks are part of post-traumatic stress symptoms.

POW: Prisoner of war. Said of soldiers who are captured in battle or while serving their country.

Socialist Republic of Vietnam: The official name of Vietnam following its reunification on July 2, 1976.

Third Force: Noncommunist Vietnamese who were opposed to the government of President Nguyen Van Thieu. These people included many Buddhist, Cao Dai, and Catholic religious leaders, plus middle-class Vietnamese.

Flamboyant Prince Norodom Sihanouk kept Cambodia free of foreign influence for more than a decade.

Index

Construction workers stage a prowar rally in New York City in 1970.

Index

Index

This antiwar rally took place in Saigon
in 1970.

North Vietnamese peasants walk on a rice paddy dike after laboring in the fields.

Acknowledgments

The series *War in Vietnam* is the product of many talented and dedicated people. Their stories, experiences, and skills helped make this series a unique contribution to our knowledge of the Vietnam era.

Author David K. Wright would like to thank the following people for their assistance: Yen Do, former Saigon resident and now a newspaper publisher in California; David Doyle, who works with resettled Hmong people from Laos; John Kuehl of the Veterans Administration; Don Luce of the Asia Resource Center in Washington, D.C.; Patricia (Kit) Norland of the Indochina Project in Washington, D.C.; John Stolting, formerly with the 9th Infantry Division Awards and Decorations Section; Frank Tatu, now with the U.S. Global Strategy Council in Washington, D.C.; Don Ehlke, a Vietnam veteran; and Donald R. Wright, a Vietnam-era veteran. These individuals gave generously of their time in personal interviews and provided resources on Southeast Asian history and current conditions.

A special thanks to Frank Burdick, Professor of History at State University College in Cortland, New York. Professor Burdick reviewed the manuscripts and made many valuable suggestions to improve them.

The editorial staff at Childrens Press who produced the four books of this series include Fran Dyra, Vice President, Editorial; Margrit Fiddle, Creative Director; L. Sue Baugh, Project Editor; Judy Feldman, Photo Editor; and Pat Stahl and Norman Zuefle, Editorial Proofreaders. Charles Hills of New Horizons & Associates created the dramatic book design for the series.

About the Author

David K. Wright is a freelance writer who lives in Wisconsin. He grew up in and around Richmond, Indiana, and graduated from Wittenberg University in Springfield, Ohio, in 1966.

Wright received his draft notice the day after he graduated from college. He was inducted in September 1966 and arrived in Vietnam at Bien Hoa in March 1967. He served in the U.S. Army 9th Infantry Division as an armor crewman. Wright was stationed at Camp Bearcat, east of Saigon, and at Dong Tam in the Mekong Delta. He returned from Vietnam in March 1968 and was honorably discharged in September of that year, having attained the rank of Specialist five.

This is the fourth in a series of four books by Wright for Childrens Press about the Vietnam War. He also has written a book on Vietnam and a book on Malaysia in the *Enchantment of the World* series also published by Childrens Press.

Picture Acknowledgments

The Bettmann Archive—Front Cover, 4-5, 8, 10, 11, 12, 17, 20, 36-37, 39, 43, 46, 47, 51, 53, 58-59, 60, 63, 71, 77, 84, 89, 92, 101, 102, 103, 104-105, 107, 108-109, 112-113, 114, 119, 131, 135, Back Cover

Black Star:
  © Lee Lockwood—64, 140-141
  © Stern/Scheler—99
  © Robert Ellison—110

Wide World Photos, Inc.—2-3, 9, 16, 18, 19, 21, 22-23, 25, 26, 27, 28-29, 30, 32, 33, 34-35, 36-37, 42, 45, 48-49, 55, 57, 65, 66-67, 68, 69, 70-71, 75, 79, 81, 82-83, 87, 93, 95, 96-97, 115, 117, 121, 123, 133, 139

Maps—15, 41, 56

Vidor High School Library
Vidor, Texas 77662

A-9875

Vidor High School Library
Vidor, Texas 77662